HAWKER
HUNTER

Hunter FGA9s of No 20 Squadron off Malaya in 1965. *MoD*

Cover: Hunter FGA9 of No 45 Squadron from RAF Wittering. *BAe Kingston*

Below: F1 WT594 was one of the original batch of Hunters allocated to
No 43 Squadron. *BAe-Kingston*

Modern Combat Aircraft 15
HAWKER
HUNTER

Robert Jackson

LONDON
IAN ALLAN LTD

First published 1982

ISBN 0 7110 1216 4

© Robert Jackson 1982

Published by Ian Allan Ltd, Shepperton, Surrey;
and printed by Ian Allan Printing Ltd at their works
at Coombelands in Runnymede, England

Contents

Left: XE531, the sole Mk 12,
with long-range tanks. Had TSR2
entered production, more Mk 12s
would have been produced for
conversion training. This nose detail
shows the bulges that housed terrain-
following radar equipment destined for
TSR2. *BAe-Kingston*

Above: WB188, the Hawker P1067 prototype, piloted by Neville Duke. *British Aerospace (BAe)-Kingston*

Below: The Hawker P1081, the aircraft that might have entered RAF service as a Meteor replacement had the Hunter not shown so much promise. *BAe-Kingston*

1
Origins of a Thoroughbred

There can be few who would dispute the claim that, when the war in Europe drew to its end in May 1945, the British aircraft industry led the world in the development of piston-engined fighter aircraft. Sadly, it is also true that before another half-decade had gone by, Britain's lead in fighter development had been stripped from her by both the United States and Soviet Russia, whose massive acquisition of German research material into high-speed flight (a race in which Britain came a poor third) made possible the speedy development and production of the two types which were to symbolise the new era of the high-performance jet fighter: the North American F-86 Sabre and the MiG-15.

During 1943-45, the development of turbojet-powered fighters in the United Kingdom was forced into the background to some degree by the need to concentrate on the refinement and production of existing piston-engined types such as the Hawker Tempest and the later marks of Spitfire — the aircraft which, after all, were winning the air war over Western Europe together with their American counterparts — and British aircraft designers were still preoccupied with a new generation of piston-engined machines, types that included the powerful Hawker Fury and the de Havilland Hornet, successor to the Mosquito in the long-range fighter role. In 1945, the Hawker Tempest V was still faster than the Gloster Meteor, Britain's first operational jet fighter, and there was no reason to suppose that piston-engined fighter types would be rendered obsolete overnight by a sudden dramatic breakthrough in turbojet engine design.

Nevertheless, the leading British aircraft companies had been tentatively studying jet-propelled projects since 1941, the year in which Britain's first reaction-propelled aircraft, the Gloster E28/39, took to the air powered by a Whittle W2/7000 jet engine, and the Hawker Aircraft Company was no exception. In 1940, Hawkers had begun preliminary design work on the P1005, a new high-speed bomber that was to have been powered by two Napier Sabre engines, and two prototypes were ordered to Air Ministry Specification B11/41 the following year; the project was cancelled in 1942, when a mock-up was almost complete, but

the Hawker Project Team considered a scheme to install a pair of Power Jet engines in the P1005 air-frame under the Company Project Designation P1011. This project never passed beyond the scheme stage, but it marked the beginning of Hawker's involvement with turbojet-powered design. Another scheme, the P1014, was also considered at about the same time; this envisaged a single-seat fighter with one Power Jet engine, but like the P1011 it remained a scheme only.

The fact that little real progress was made in the jet aircraft field at this time was due in the main to the unsuitability of the early Power Jet engines, which were bulky in design and which had far too low a power output to offer even a comparable performance to that of contemporary piston engines. However, by 1943 considerable refinements had been made in turbojet design, and in that year the Hawker Company began to consider new schemes, this time based on jet engines then being developed by Rolls-Royce. The first of these was the P1031, a scheme for a jet fighter powered by a Rolls-Royce B40 engine; this powerplant, and the further refined B41, was smaller and lighter than previous turbojets and offered considerably more power potential, and in 1944 the Hawker Project Team embarked on a preliminary design study to mount a B41 engine in an existing air-frame, the Hawker Fury, under the project designation P1035.

Other projects based on the B41 which the Hawker team considered in 1944 were the P1034 (the P1005 bomber project with two B41s), the P1038 and the P1039, both of which were also based on the P1005 but which envisaged different methods of mounting the engines — in the fuselage, for example, in the case of the P1039.

It was the P1035 project, however, on which the main design effort was focused, and the Ministry of Aircraft Production showed a good deal of interest in it during the summer of 1944. Following the preliminary design work, more detailed proposals were submitted in December 1944, by which time the original P1035 proposal had undergone numerous changes. The B41 engine, which was situated in the fuselage immediately aft of the cockpit, was fed by two air intakes built into the wing roots, and in their quest to keep the tail pipe as short as possible to cut down thrust losses the Hawker design team came up with the novel idea of a split, or bifurcated, jet pipe that exhausted on either side of the fuselage just aft of the engine.

In its new guise the P1035 became the P1040, and work on the detail design of a prototype progressed as a private venture during the winter of 1944-45, Hawkers collaborating closely with Rolls-Royce on the marriage of the powerplant to the airframe. In February 1945 design work was sufficiently advanced to enable the Hawker Company to submit a firm tender to the Air Ministry, but no specification was forthcoming and as the year went by the interest of the Air Staff gradually waned, although the Naval Staff showed growing enthusiasm for the project as a possible replacement for the Royal Navy's piston-engined fleet fighters. In October 1945 the Company decided to go ahead and build the aircraft as a private venture, and a Production Order was issued for the manufacture of one prototype, VP401.

Shortly afterwards, the Air Staff — influenced by the performance of the Gloster Meteor Mk 4, which in November 1945 had set up a world speed record of 606.25mph at Herne Bay — announced that it no longer supported the P1040 project as a future RAF jet fighter. The disappointment felt by the Hawker team was keen, but in January 1946 the P1040 design was revamped a little and submitted to the Admiralty as a naval interceptor. The Naval Staff accepted the proposal and Specification N7/46 was written around it, Hawkers receiving an Instruction to Proceed on the building of three flying prototypes and one for static testing. The P1040 prototype, VP401, flew for the first time on 2 September 1947, and in its production guise it became the Sea Hawk.

Meanwhile, in October 1945, as construction of the P1040 was about to begin, Hawker Aircraft Ltd has also begun limited design studies of a variant known as the P1047, which was basically a P1040 fuselage featuring a wing swept at an angle of 35 degrees and powered by a rocket motor. This was schemed only, but the Royal Aircraft Establishment showed considerable interest in the swept-wing proposal and during 1946, following discussions with Hawker, Supermarine and the Ministry of Supply, two Specifications were prepared, each calling for the construction of a research aircraft to investigate different approaches to transonic flight. The Specification issued to Supermarine, E1/46, resulted in the Supermarine 510, which featured 40 degrees of sweepback and eventually led to the Swift; that issued to Hawker Aircraft Ltd, on 16 January 1947, called for an aircraft with 35 degrees of sweep at quarter-chord. Both designs were to have a thickness/chord ratio of 10%.

In March 1947 Hawkers submitted their tender to meet Specification E38/46, which had been written around the 35-degree sweep proposal; this was accepted, and two months later the Company received a contract for the construction of two prototypes. The Company designation was P1052, and the serials allocated were VX272 and VX279.

Both P1052s were built at the new Hawker factory in Richmond Road, Kingston, and VX272 flew for the first time on 19 November 1948. By June 1949 both prototypes were fully engaged in a high-speed research programme, furnishing much valuable information for

both Hawker Aircraft Ltd and the RAE. The performance of the P1052, in fact, showed such promise that at one point, late in 1948, it was seriously proposed to place the type in quantity production for the Royal Air Force as a replacement for the Gloster Meteor, but other fighter designs which were then on the drawing board showed even greater potential and the idea was dropped.

The need for more modern fighter aircraft to replace the Meteor in the day-fighter role and the piston-engined Mosquito as the RAF's standard night-fighter had crystallised in two Specifications, F43/46 and F44/46, both issued by the Air Staff in 1946. Both specifications, however, were based on shaky foundations; knowledge of high speed flight parameters was then insufficient to project the requirements for a new RAF day fighter satisfactorily, and no agreement could be reached on the optimum armament for such an aircraft, while the Specification for a night fighter resulted in what was at best a compromise, the Meteor NF11.

Nevertheless, during 1947 Hawker Aircraft Ltd undertook numerous investigations in an attempt to find a solution to the F43/46 requirement. The most promising line of research appeared to involve a design based on the new Rolls-Royce AJ65 turbojet, which was later to become the Avon and which had an initial thrust rating of 6,500lb, giving it approximately the same power as the Meteor's twin Derwents. Sydney Camm's design team therefore set about designing a day fighter built around this engine, although the original F43/46 specification had called for a twin-engined machine, and in January 1948 they submitted their ideas to the Air Ministry under the project designation P1067.

In March 1948 the Air Ministry issued a new Specification, F3/48, which conformed to the Air Staff's Operational Requirement 228. The latter called for a single-seat fighter landplane for day interception duties in any part of the world; its primary role would be the interception of high-speed, high-altitude bombers as soon as possible after radar detection, and it would also have a secondary ground attack role. The highest importance was attached to speed and rate of climb, the requirement calling for a maximum speed in level flight of at least 547kts at 45,000ft; it would also be desirable to have a diving speed of at least 1.2M. The time from engine start to 45,000ft, including taxy time, was not to exceed six minutes, while the rate of climb was to be not less than 1,000ft/min at 50,000ft. The required endurance was one-and-a-quarter hours, including climb to 45,000ft and 10 minutes' combat at full power at that height. The take-off distance to clear 50ft was not to exceed 1,200yd in still-air conditions, with a similar requirement for the landing run.

The original design worked up by Hawkers to meet

Top left: Nose construction detail of WB188. *BAe-Kingston*

Above: The original configuration of the Hunter's airbrakes was at the side — as seen here on WB188 in modified form. *BAe-Kingston*

Left: Construction of Hunter prototypes at Hawker's Kingston factory on the Richmond Road. *BAe-Kingston*

Bottom left: The P1067's Aden gun pack in position. *BAe-Kingston*

Below: Detail of an early Hunter's fire control radar. *BAe-Kingston*

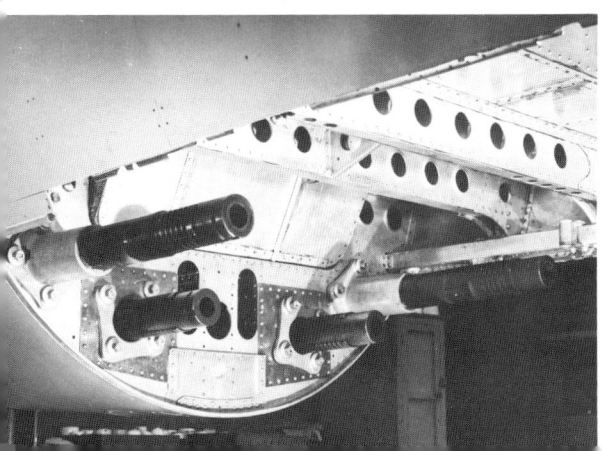

the old F43/46 requirement was a single-seat aircraft with an all-up weight of 12,000lb, the AJ65 turbojet being fed through a nose intake. All flying surfaces were swept at a 40-degree angle and the design featured a tailplane mounted on top of the fin. The airframe was to be of all-metal stressed-skin construction, and the proposed armament was two 30mm cannon. After the issue of F3/48, however, this basic design was altered somewhat; following a series of aerodynamic wind tunnel tests the tailplane was moved to a new position down the fin, while a requirement to install new radar equipment in the nose led to the adoption of wing root intakes similar to those developed for the P1040 and P1052. A much bolder step was the decision to adopt an armament of four 30mm Aden cannon, mounted below the cockpit floor in a detachable pack specially developed by the Hawker design team, an arrangement that enabled the four gun bodies and their magazines to be winched down on to a special trolley, removed quickly and replaced by a fully loaded pack. Each magazine held 130 rounds (later increased to 150) and the Aden gun's rate of fire of 1,200 rounds/min meant that the Hawker design would carry a punch that was potentially eight times greater than that of fighter aircraft equipped with the 20mm Hispano cannon. The devastating effect of four 30mm cannon had been demonstrated in 1944-45, when such armament had been used by the Messerschmitt Me262 against American daylight bombers, but the P1067 was the first British fighter to be so equipped. As well as the detachable gun pack — which weighed about 2,000lb — the P1067 had a single refuelling point in the port wheel bay, giving it the potential to be refuelled and rearmed in less than eight minutes between combat sorties.

For ease of servicing, the P1067's airframe was divided into six fully interchangeable major components: the fuselage nose section comprising the cockpit, armament pack and nosewheel; the fuselage centre section with integral wing roots, engine mounts and intake ducting; detachable rear fuselage section with integral fin base and removable jet pipe and tail cone; and the tail unit and mainplanes, complete with main undercarriage members. A necessary requirement for high-g manoeuvring at high speed was the provision of power-operated ailerons and elevator, the power being supplied by hydraulic pressure to the aileron and elevator hydroboosters, but the pilot could select manual operation by releasing a switch in the cockpit. The control column/aileron gearing was automatically changed when manual reversion occurred, so that for the same stick movement aileron travel in Manual was about two-thirds of that obtained in Power. The design also incorporate an electrically-operated variable-incidence tailplane to trim out the

changes of stick force; the main motor was controlled by a thumb switch on top of the stick and the tailplane operated in the same way as a conventional trimming tab, although much more powerfully. An electrical interconnection enabled the variable-incidence tailplane to follow up the movement of the elevator, permitting much greater manoeuvrability at high Mach numbers when used together.

The P1067's cockpit was fully pressurised, hot air under pressure being bled off from the engine compressor to supply the heating, pressurisation and demisting system. Cockpit layout was straightforward and the pilot was provided with a Martin-Baker ejection seat.

A mock-up of the new P1067, incorporating all the latest refinements, was begun in September 1948, and an order for three prototypes was placed by the Ministry of Supply in November. Two of these, WB188 and WB195, were to be powered by Rolls-Royce Avon engines, while the third, WB202, was to be fitted with an Armstrong-Siddeley Sapphire (the engine that had been selected to power the Gloster Javelin all-weather fighter, on which much of the RAF's defence burden would rest from the mid-1950s) mainly as an insurance against problems and delays that might be experienced with the Avon.

By the end of 1949 construction of the jigs for the first prototype was well under way, and the P1067's nose section was virtually complete by the beginning of April 1950. Some unexpected delay occurred in May, when the Ministry of Supply suddenly decided that the provision of an armament of four 30mm Aden cannon might produce too great a weight penalty and briefly considered reducing it to two 30mm or four 20mm weapons, but soon afterwards there was a further change of mind and work went ahead once more, construction of the other two prototypes now having started also.

On 20 October 1950, Hawker Aircraft Ltd received an Instruction to Proceed with production planning for 200 Avon-powered aircraft, while a further 200 Sapphire-powered machines were to be built by Sir W. G. Armstrong Whitworth Aircraft Ltd at Coventry. One hundred and thirty-nine of the Avon-powered aircraft were to emerge as the Hunter F Mk 1, while the Sapphire-powered machines were to enter RAF service as the Hunter Mks 2 and 5.

By the spring of 1951 the first prototype P1067 — or Hunter, as the type was now officially known — was beginning to take very definite shape, and as the final jobs were started, such as wing and fuselage skinning, wiring, control system functioning, engine installation and fuel system testing, the tension at Kingston rose sharply. This hectic period of anticipation was marred, in April 1951, by the death of Hawkers' Chief Test Pilot, Sqn Ldr T. S. 'Wimpy'

Wade DFC, AFC, who was killed while flying the Hawker P1081 — the second P1052, VX279, which had been fitted with a Rolls-Royce Tay engine in response to an enquiry by the Australian Government, who were showing interest in an operational version. Wade was succeeded by Sqn Ldr Neville Duke DSO, DFC, who had a distinguished career as a fighter pilot during the war and who, before joining Hawkers in 1948, had been a RAF test pilot at the A&AEE, Boscombe Down.

To prepare himself for flying the Hunter, Duke flew a Canberra with Avon engines to get experience of handling this powerplant, and to acquire experience of transonic flight he also flew a North American F-86 Sabre. In June, the first prototype Hunter, WB188, was moved from Kingston to Boscombe Down, which had a 3,000yd runway, and for the next three weeks the Hawker engineering team carried out prolonged running tests on the Avon engine, ensuring that there was no overheating of the airframe around the engine and jet pipe. All proved satisfactory, and Duke was cleared to start taxying trials. After a series of slow taxying, during which he tested the Hunter's manoeuvrability on the ground, he began to move progressively faster along Boscombe's runway, checking for shimmy and brake snatching and gradually working up to speeds at which the nosewheel came clear of the ground and the elevators and rudder became effective.

The taxying trials culminated in a short hop, enabling the pilot to get the feel of the controls and to determine the correct unstick speed and trimmer setting. The hop was completely satisfactory, but the Hunter had covered a lot of runway by the time it touched down again and Duke was forced to brake sharply, slewing the aircraft round on to the perimeter track. The tyres were ruined and the brakes completely burned out, but after replacements were fitted more taxying trials were carried out, and during the week that followed there were further engine runs and a good many final adjustments in preparation for the Hunter's maiden flight.

Duke finally took WB188 into the air for the first time in the evening of 20 July 1951. The aircraft, which was painted a pale, duck-egg green overall, carried no armament and was fitted with a spin recovery parachute in a fairing at the base of the fin. Duke went up to 20,000ft over the south coast and put the prototype through its paces for an hour before returning to Boscombe to make an effortless landing and announce to a crowd of jubilant Hawker employees that their three years of effort had been worthwhile, and that all was well.

Duke flew the Hunter half a dozen more times from Boscombe, then took the aircraft over to the Hawker airfield at Dunsfold to begin the development pro-

Above: Tail view of WB188 showing bullet fairings and anti-spin parachute fitted. *BAe-Kingston*

gramme. Further flight trials produced comparatively few snags, and these were only of a minor nature, so the aircraft was cleared to appear at the 1951 SBAC Show at Farnborough in September. After Farnborough, the flight development programme continued at every opportunity whenever the weather was favourable, the aircraft gradually being flown higher and faster until, in April 1952, Duke exceeded Mach unity in WB188.

In May 1952 the flight test programme was joined by the second Avon-powered Hunter prototype, WB195, which made its first flight on the 3rd of that month. This aircraft was fully armed with the Aden gun pack and was equipped with gun ranging radar, representative of production aircraft. By this time the Hunter had been ordered into 'super-priority' production for the Royal Air Force and Hawkers had an order for an initial production batch of 113 aircraft, placed with the company on 14 March 1951.

The third, Sapphire-powered, Hunter prototype, WB202, flew for the first time on 30 November 1952, and large-scale tooling-up for the production of both Avon- and Sapphire-powered variants continued at Kingston and Coventry during 1952, although the Hunter orders in general were subjected to some fluctuation; for example, the order for 200 Sapphire-powered machines was cut down to 150, 45 of these eventually emerging as Hunter F2s and the remainder as F5s.

The first production Avon-powered Hunter F1,

Top: WB188, with Neville Duke at the controls, shows its graceful lines in plan view. *BAe-Kingston*

Above: WB195, the second Avon-powered P1067 prototype. *BAe-Kingston*

Right: Assembling WB202, the third (Sapphire-powered) Hunter prototype at Hawker's Richmond Road works. *BAe-Kingston*

WT555, flew for the first time on 16 May 1953 from Dunsfold, powered by a 7,500lb st Rolls-Royce Avon 100 series turbojet. This aircraft was retained by Hawker Aircraft Ltd for handling trials, while the next four went to the A&AEE at Boscombe Down — WT556 for familiarisation, WT557 for radio trials, WT558 for gun firing trials and WT559 for various tests involving canopy emergency release. In all, 23 aircraft from the initial Hunter F1 production batch were used for a variety of trials by either Hawker Aircraft, the A&AEE, the RAE or Rolls-Royce.

By the end of 1953 Hunter production orders totalled 600 aircraft, but there was some delay before the first Hunter F1s were delivered to the RAF while the air brake arrangement on production aircraft was revised. During prototype testing, it had been found that the operation of the original wing-mounted air brakes caused marked attitude changes under rapid combat deceleration conditions; several experimental braking surfaces were tested, eventually resulting in the fitting of a large 'barn door' air brake under the rear fuselage, and this was to be a feature of all production Hunters. The air brake was electrically selected by means of a three-position switch positioned on the throttle lever and hydraulically operated, being designed to extend fully at any speed. As a built-in safeguard, the air brake automatically became inoperative when the undercarriage was lowered, and if the pilot inadvertently selected gear down with the brake out, the latter automatically retracted.

Meanwhile, exhaustive trials of the aircraft allocated from the first production batch continued at Hawkers and the various Ministry establishments. Aircraft so employed included WT563, which was fitted with an interim flying tail; WT564, which saw a lot of flying with the A&AEE as interception target aircraft; WT566, which was used to develop the new air brake; WT568, which was used for extended wing leading

Below: WT555, the first production Avon-powered Hunter F1. This aircraft was retained by HAL for handling trials. *BAe-Kingston*

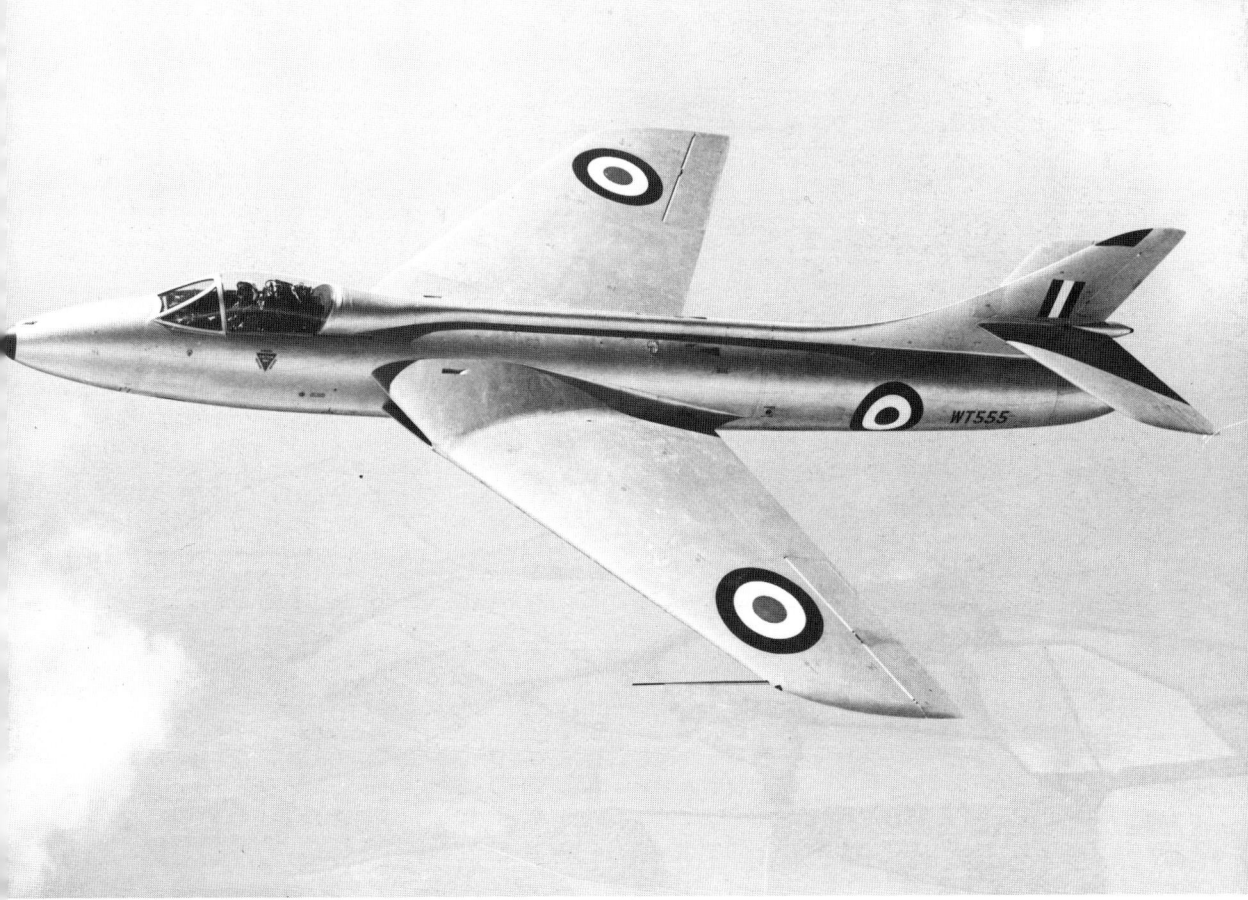

edge trials by the A&AEE; and WT571, an interesting RAE modification featuring an area-ruled rear fuselage.

The experiences of the RAF test pilots at Boscombe Down and elsewhere, consolidating the findings of the Hawker flight test team, showed the Hunter F1 to be a viceless, robust aircraft that was crisp and responsive to fly. The 'g' limitations imposed on the airframe were $+7$ and $-3\frac{3}{4}$, quite adequate for all likely air combat manoeuvres at that time; the aircraft's maximum speed with power controls operative was 620kts and there was no Mach limit, although maximum speed in level flight at full throttle was 0.93 to 0.95M. As the speed increased to about 0.90M there was a progressive nose-up change of trim, followed by a nose-down change and then another nose-up change between 0.90M and 0.94M, until at 0.96M the aircraft was relatively stable once more.

From 40,000ft and above the Hunter F1 was found to be capable of exceeding sonic speed in a 30 to 40 degree dive at full throttle. If the dive angle was too shallow the aircraft would only reach a maximum speed of 0.97M. Apart from a very slight wing drop, easily counteracted by the use of aileron, there were no problems in taking the Hunter through the transonic regime.

Taxying the Hunter F1 was normal as for any other nosewheel aircraft, with fuel consumption about 15lb per minute while taxying. There was no tendency to swing on take-off, the rudder becoming effective at about 90kts. The nosewheel came off the ground at 120kts and unstick speed was in the order of 150kts, depending on weight and prevailing conditions. The best rate of climb was 430kts until 0.85M was reached, this Mach value being maintained thereafter; the rate of climb dropped away rapidly above 30,000ft if the speed was allowed to fall below 0.85M. At 0.85M, a climb from sea level to 45,000ft took approximately 14 minutes, the Hunter covering a horizontal distance of 99 nautical miles and the time taken from wheels rolling. The rate of descent was rapid, the aircraft losing 45,000ft in just over seven minutes.

Because of this fast rate of descent, and also because it was possible to induce an inadvertent spin when the aircraft was fully stalled, stalling restrictions were placed on the Hunter F1 (and, indeed, on subsequent marks), in that stalling practice was not to be carried out below 25,000ft and then only up to the pre-stall buffet stage. With undercarriage and flap up, the stall occurred at between 135 and 140kts, depending on weight, and 125kts with undercarriage down and full flap. Intentional spinning was permitted provided that the spin was started at not less than 40,000ft and recovery action initiated before completion of the fourth turn or, in the case of a slow spin,

Above: WB202, the Sapphire-powered prototype, nearing completion. *BAe-Kingston*

Above right: WT557, the F1 used by A&AEE for radio trials, tucks into the Meteor chase aircraft. *BAe-Kingston*

Right: WT571, the Hunter Mk 1 used by the RAF for area-rule trials — the bulged fairings can be seen at the rear of the aircraft. *BAe-Kingston*

Far right: The prototype WB188 in all-red, record-breaking guise. Known as the Hunter Mk 3, WB188 set a new world air speed record at the hands of Neville Duke on 7 September 1951 — 727.63mph. *BAe-Kingston*

by 25,000ft. The recommended entry speed from a stall was 120kts, and from a turn 200kts. Rate of descent in the spin was about 24,000ft/min.

Circuit and landing in the Hunter presented no problems, the circuit usually being joined at 170-180kts with 23 degrees of flap. The crosswind turn on to final approach was made at 160kts, with 130-135kts the recommended speed over the threshold. The drill was to fly the aircraft gently on to the ground at about 5-10kts less than the threshold speed, as holding off could result in a marked nose-up attitude with the attendant danger of a wing dropping as the tail cone scraped the runway.

The most serious problem encountered during handling and Service acceptance trials with the Hunter F1 was the tendency of the Avon 113 engine to surge and flame out when the cannon armament was fired at high altitude, the result of shock waves entering the air intakes. Rolls-Royce worked hard to find a solution, and before Hunter F1 production was completed

modified Avons with a fuel-dipping system were being introduced, but in the early months of 1954, with the Hunter's service debut eagerly awaited, the problem still remained unsolved, and as a consequence an altitude restriction was placed on cannon firing with this early mark.

Meanwhile, in the summer of the previous year, a Hunter had made aviation history. Not long after the first production Hunter had flown, Hawkers had married the airframe of the prototype P1067, WB188, to an afterburning Rolls-Royce Avon RA7R turbojet developing 7,130lb st and 9,600lb with reheat; other modifications included a more streamlined nose and cockpit windscreen, a clamshell-type jet pipe nozzle and rear fuselage air brakes, the aircraft being involved in air brake trials at the time. Known as the Hunter Mk 3 in its new guise, WB188 was flown by Neville Duke over a three-kilometre course off Rustington, near Littlehampton on the south coast of Sussex, to set up a new World Absolute Speed Record of 727.6mph

on 7 September 1963. On 19 September, Duke followed up this exploit by taking the aircraft — painted bright red to facilitate camera tracking — round a 100km closed circuit at an average speed of 709.2mph, setting up another world record.

After these record-breaking attempts, WB188 returned to trials work with Hawker Aircraft Ltd, afterwards being sold to the Ministry of Supply in 1955. Its flying days over, it was statically displayed at RAF Stations Halton, Melksham, Colerne and St Athan.

Taking into account the performance of this aircraft with reheat, it seems strange on reflection that the Air Staff's uncompromising attitude towards afterburning turbojets during the early 1950s showed no change, and that emphasis remained firmly on the development of large 'dry' jet engines throughout the Hunter series. Had later marks of Hunter been equipped with reheat, it is probable that the aircraft's overseas sales potential would have been considerably increased.

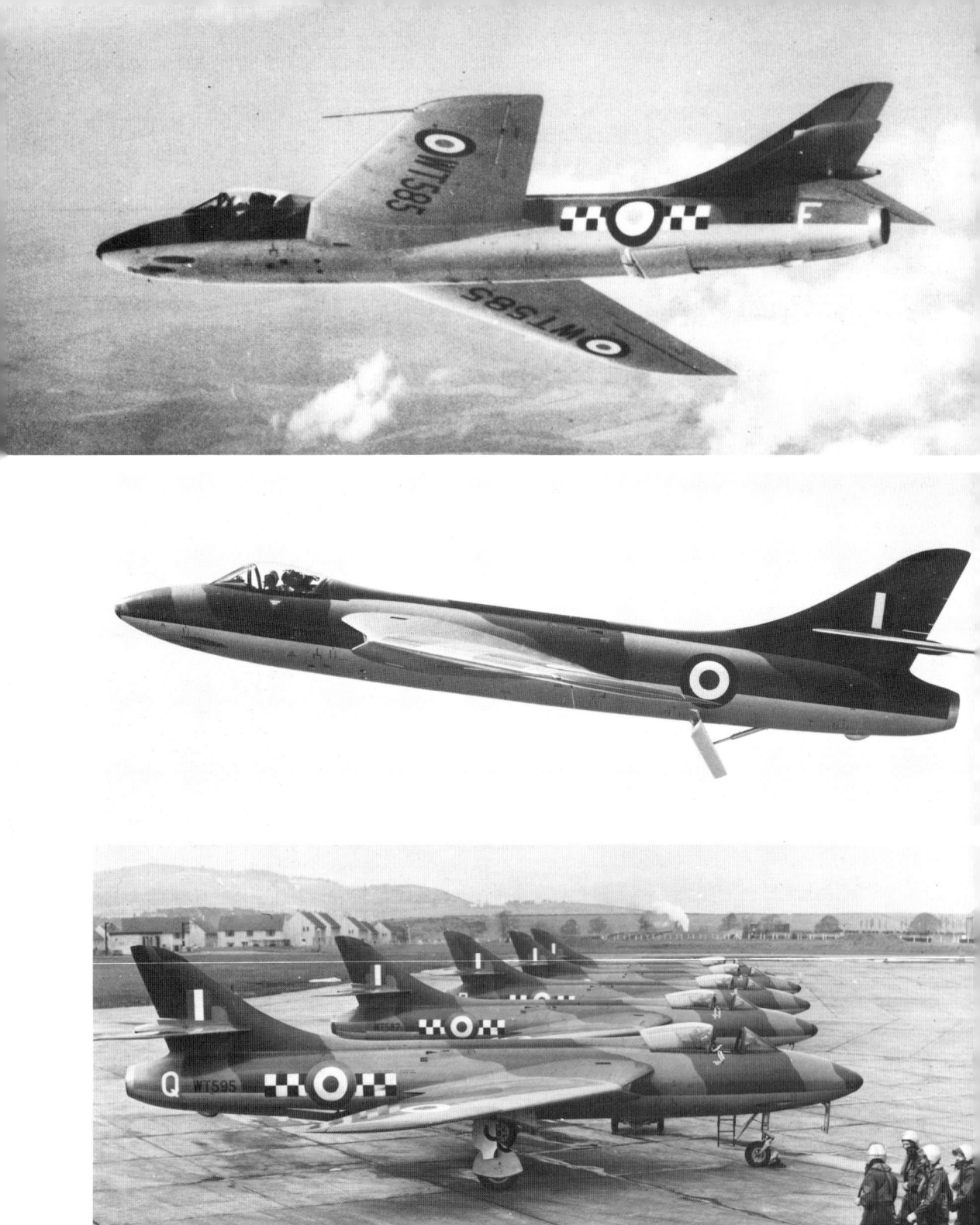

2
RAF Service and Further Development

Hunter F Mk 1 and F Mk 2

In July 1954 three Hunter F Mk 1s, WT576, WT577 and WT578, were allocated to the Air Fighting Development Squadron at West Raynham, this becoming the first RAF unit to receive the type. The Hunters were subjected to a period of intensive flying, including participation in Exercise 'Dividend', during which they carried out practice interceptions of Canberras, B-45s and B-47s at altitudes of up to 40,000ft. Also in July, the first Hunter F1s were allocated to No 43 Squadron at Leuchars, in Scotland, and it was during operations with this unit that the restriction on cannon firing at high altitude came into force following a spate of 'flame outs'.

The trouble experienced by the Hunter F1 in this respect followed hard on the heels of much more serious snags encountered with the service debut of the RAF's other transonic jet fighter, the Supermarine Swift, which had entered service with No 56 Squadron in February 1954. Both the Swift F1 and F2 were found to be unsuitable for their intended role of high-altitude interception, being prone to tightening in turns and suffering frequent flame outs as a result of shock

Top left: WT585, an early F1 allocated to No 43 Squadron, Leuchars; note ventral airbrake. *BAe-Kingston*

Centre left: F1 WT594 was one of the original batch of Hunters allocated to No 43 Squadron. This fine air-to-air view shows the working of the ventral airbrake. *BAe-Kingston*

Bottom left: No 43 Squadron Hunter F1s at Leuchars in 1955. *MoD*

Right: Hunter F1s of No 43 Squadron, RAF Leuchars, in 1955. The No 4 aircraft in the formation belonged to the Day Fighter Leaders' School and is not fitted with ammunition link collectors. *MoD*

waves entering the intakes when the nose armament was fired. By February 1955, the Air Ministry had decided that the Swift could not be relied upon to carry out its primary role, and its day as an interceptor was at an end, although in its low-level fighter reconnaissance variant it served for five years with two RAF squadrons in Germany. The Swift's demise provided an enormous boost for the Hunter's prospects, for at the beginning of 1955 the latter was designated as Fighter Command's standard day fighter, now being scheduled to equip those interceptor squadrons which should have used the Supermarine type.

The second squadron to equip with the Hunter F1, in December 1954, was No 222, which was also based at Leuchars; it was followed, in February 1955, by No 54 Squadron at Odiham in Hampshire. These were the only three squadrons to use the Hunter F1, but 25 F1s were allocated to No 229 Operational Conversion Unit at Chivenor in Devon, which in 1955 was beginning to turn out a steady stream of qualified Hunter pilots. Before its Hunter days, No 229 had been the OCU for Fighter Command's and 2nd Tactical Air Force's F-86 Sabre pilots, so its instructors already had considerable experience of high-speed, high-altitude operations. Later, in 1956, a second Hunter OCU, No 233, was formed at Pembrey in South Wales to assist No 229 in coping with the

large numbers of Hunter pilots required as more Fighter Command squadrons equipped with the type; No 233 OCU used about 20 Hunter F1s, many of them released from the front-line squadrons as the latter re-equipped with F4s.

Meanwhile, in November 1954, No 257 Squadron at Wattisham, in Suffolk, had become the first to equip with the Sapphire-engined Hunter F Mk 2, and in January 1955 F2s were also issued to the other Wattisham-based unit, No 263 Squadron. The Sapphire engine was not prone to high-altitude flame out during gun firing, as was the early Avon series 113/114, and working up to operational standard on the new type was uneventful. Apart from Nos 257 and 263 Squadrons, the only other RAF units to operate F2s were the Air Fighting Development Squadron, which used five examples, and No 1 Squadron, which in April 1955 received one F2, WN919, for conversion training pending the arrival of Hunter F5s, which were also Sapphire-powered. One F2, WN891, was sent to Canada for cold weather trials in the winter of 1954-55.

The Hunter Mks 1 and 2, although they served with only five squadrons and were severely limited operationally by their short endurance, nevertheless filled a dangerous gap in Fighter Command's air defences at a time when fighter requirements were undergoing profound changes as a result of the lessons learned during the Korean War — one of which was that the Gloster Meteor, which still equipped the bulk of Fighter Command's squadrons early in 1955, was badly outclassed by the MiG-15. The Hunters 1 and 2 were essentially interim aircraft, and despite all their shortcomings (in the case of the Mk 1 at least) they enabled the RAF to become acclimatised to the new type while the Service awaited the introduction of a new variant that was more closely compatible with the Air Staff's original Operational Requirement No 228.

Hunter F Mk 4

In 1954, Hawker Aircraft Ltd had flown a Hunter 1 with trial drop tank installations, and for incorporation in later marks the Hawker Design Team developed a modified fuel system, increasing the internal tankage as well as providing underwing attachments for two 100gal Bristol drop tanks and strengthening the wing structure to permit the installation of leading edge tanks. Underwing hard points were also provided for a variety of external stores to fit the Hunter for its secondary ground-attack role, as required by OR228.

These modifications were incorporated in the 114th Hunter to come off the Kingston production line

(WT701) and the 27th machine to be built at Blackpool (WW646), these and subsequent Hunters bearing the designation F Mk 4. Production of the Mk 4, which was shared between Kingston and Blackpool, was eventually to total 365 aircraft. First Service deliveries were made to No 54 (F) Squadron at Odiham in March 1955, the unit's F1s being allocated to the OCUs and to various training establishments, and in June 1955 the new mark was also issued to No 111 (F) Squadron at North Weald, replacing that unit's Meteor 8s. 'Treble One' got off to a fine start with the Hunter when, on 8 August 1955, its commanding officer set up a new Edinburgh-London speed record in Mk 4 WT739 'R', with an average speed of 714.504mph; the Squadron had set up an earlier record in February 1938, having then just become the first RAF unit to equip with Hurricanes. In the late 1950s, the Hurricane's transonic successor was to bring 111 Squadron international fame as the RAF's official aerobatic team, eventually known as the 'Black Arrows', and no one who saw those impeccable formation displays — building up in the end to an aerobatic routine by no fewer than 22 Hunters — will ever forget them.

The Hunter F Mk 4 eventually equipped 22 RAF fighter squadrons in both Fighter Command and the 2nd Tactical Air Force, in the front line of NATO's air defences. Thirteen of the 22 F4 squadrons, in fact, were based in Germany, where the Hunter replaced either the Sabre F1/F4 or the de Havilland Venom, and these formed four Fighter Wings, with Nos 3 and 234 Squadrons at Geilenkirchen, Nos 4, 93, 98 and 118 Squadrons at Jever, Nos 14, 20 and 26 Squadrons at Oldenburg and Nos 67, 71, 112 and 130 Squadrons at Bruggen. At home, apart from Nos 54 and 111 Squadrons, the Hunter F4 equipped Nos 43 and 222 Squadrons at Leuchars, Nos 66 and 92 Squadrons at Linton-on-Ouse, No 245 Squadron at Horsham St Faith and No 247 Squadron at Odiham.

Although the early Hunter 4s still suffered from

Below and right: XF310, the Fireflash AAM trials Hunter, at different stages of the tests — note the modified nose *(right)*. BAe-Kingston

engine surge problems at altitude, the first 156 machines still using the Avon 113 engine, subsequent aircraft were fitted with the modified Avon 115, and in fact the majority of the earlier aircraft were retrospectively modified. The Hunter 4 was also the first mark to be fitted with ammunition link containers under the nose; this modification was found to be necessary after it was found that ejected links were sometimes sucked into the air intakes.

Early Hunter Mk 4s were equipped with inboard stores pylons only; these could carry 100gal drop tanks, 500lb bombs, 1,000lb bombs, napalm or practice bombs. Later, Modification 228 made provision for the carriage of outboard stores in the form of either 100gal drop tanks or 2in rocket projectiles. Much work involving trial installations of underwing stores was undertaken at Dunsfold during 1955-56, the principal 'workhorse' being WT703, the third production Mk 4. Drop tank trials were also carried out with the first production aircraft, WT701.

Two more interesting Mk 4s used for trials work were WT780 and XF310. The former was used to test a Plessey ram-air turbine, installed in the starboard side of the rear fuselage, as part of the system associated with a projected slab tailplane; after the tailplane was cancelled in 1956 WT780 was fitted with five nose cameras and, under the designation FR Mk 4, was submitted to the Air Ministry to meet Specification FR164D. In the event, this Specification was met by the fighter-reconnaissance variants of the Swift, and after its cameras were removed WT780

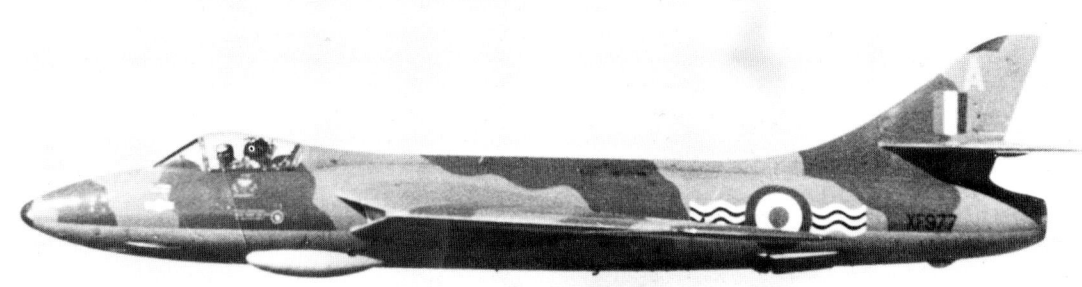

became a film star, being leased to a film company to play the leading non-human part in 'High Flight', which followed the career of young RAF officers from their days at Cranwell to operational flying on a Hunter squadron.

The other trials Hunter 4, XF310, was extensively modified to carry two Fairey Fireflash beam-riding AAMs under the wings and was equipped with missile fire-control radar in a lengthened nose. After undergoing a successful programme of test firings, mainly over the Llanbedr range in Wales, XF310 went back to Hawkers for conversion to a T7 two-seater in 1958.

The Mk 4 Hunter proved an immensely popular aircraft in RAF service, its powered controls making it crisp and responsive to handle throughout the flight regime, and serviceability was generally high. The Hunter was not a simple aircraft to service in some respects and was certainly the most complex fighter the RAF had operated so far, but its rapid turn-round time between sorties compensated for other difficulties, and it was certainly a less complex and more robust aircraft than the Sabre F1 and F4, which it replaced in

several 2nd TAF and two Fighter Command squadrons.

The 2nd TAF Hunter squadrons were generally more hard-worked than their Fighter Command counterparts; their primary task was border interception, and with the East German frontier only a few miles from their bases there was little time to relax. Each wing maintained a Duty Battle Flight at all times; this consisted of one squadron, with one pair of Hunters on immediate standby and the rest on 15 minutes' readiness. In time of war, the whole 2nd TAF fighter force had to be in the air within one hour of the alert sounding. To keep the squadrons on top line general alert practices could be called at any time of the day or night, and in that event the aircraft on immediate readiness had to be airborne within 35 seconds of receiving the alert. High-level interception training went on all the time, with either Hunter v Hunter or Hunter v Venom. There were some very tight Hunter/Venom practice combats, because at high altitude — 45,000ft or more — the twin-boom de Havilland fighter-bomber could easily out-turn the

Hunter, and the latter did not always emerge the victor.

The Hunter squadrons in Germany were often scrambled towards the eastern border to investigate suspect aircraft, but these usually turned out to be RB-57 Canberras returning from reconnaissance missions or other friendly types. From 1956, Hunter pilots in Germany reported being mystified by their failure to intercept certain unidentified aircraft cruising on lone unspecified missions thousands of feet above the Hunter's ceiling; only later did they learn that these were Lockheed U-2s, flying reconnaissance sorties deep into the Soviet Union. Apart from practice and actual interceptions, the 2nd TAF Hunter squadrons carried out a lot of air-to-air and air-to-ground firing on detachments to the Weapons Training Unit on the island of Sylt, and there were regular exchanges with squadrons of other NATO air forces to ensure that joint training and handling procedures were kept up to date.

The Hunter Mk 4 remained in first-line service with the RAF until 1957, when it began to be replaced by the Mk 6, after which it rendered valuable service for some time longer with 229 OCU (233 OCU having now disbanded) and with Advanced Flying Schools. Many examples became two-seat trainer conversions, and some of those sold to or licence-built by overseas air forces (see Hunter exports) were later returned to Hawkers for refurbishing and resale in the 1960s.

Hunter F Mk 5

The first Hunter F Mk 5, WN954, flew on 19 October 1954, a day earlier than the first Hawker-built Mk 4. This aircraft was in fact the 46th F2 to come off Armstrong-Whitworth's production line at Coventry, but incorporating modifications similar to those of the F4 — a greater fuel capacity and wing strong points for stores. The Hunter 5 used the same engine as the F2, an Armstrong-Siddeley Sapphire Mk 101, and first deliveries were made to No 1 Squadron in September 1955. Thanks to the availability of Hunter F2 WN919, which had been allocated to the Squadron in April 1955 for conversion training, No 1 quickly reached full operational status with the F5 and took part in the air exercises which were held in October that year.

During 1956 five more squadrons also equipped with the Hunter F5; these were No 34, which formed the Tangmere Wing together with No 1; No 41, which in the mid-1950s was the only regular fighter squadron (and the last) to be based at the famous wartime airfield of Biggin Hill; No 56 at Waterbeach; and Nos 257 and 263 at Wattisham.

In October 1956, the Mk 5s of Nos 1 and 34 Squadrons were hurriedly deployed to Akrotiri, in Cyprus, in support of the airborne phase of Operation 'Musketeer', the Anglo-French seizure of keypoints on the Suez Canal. The Hunters flew top cover for RAF and Fleet Air Arm fighter-bombers during the first series of daylight attacks, but their limited endurance did not permit a useful period over the target and, in view of the fact that no opposition was encountered, they were thereafter employed on quick-reaction CAP duty in protection of the Cyprus bases until their return to the United Kingdom in December.

The squadrons began to relinquish their Mk 5s in 1957. The first to go was No 257, which disbanded on 29 March that year, and it was followed by No 263 in October. On 10 January 1958 No 34 Squadron disbanded, many of its personnel remaining at Tangmere to form No 208 Squadron with Hunter F6s, and No 41 also disbanded before the end of January, to be renumbered No 141 Squadron with Gloster Javelin FAW4s. No 1 Squadron disbanded in June 1958 but reformed on 1 July by renumbering 263 Squadron at Stradishall, the unit now operating Hunter F6s. The last squadron to give up its F5s was No 56, which re-equipped with F6s late in 1958. The ex-squadron Hunter F5s were placed in storage at Colerne, from where some were repurchased by Hawkers and stored at Langley against the possibility of resale to overseas customers.

WN958, the Sapphire-powered Mk 5 used by the A&AEE for external stores trials, carrying drop tanks and RPs. *BAe-Kingston*

Hunter F Mk 6

The F6 version of the Hunter owed its origins to the cancellation of the Hawker P1083, a planned supersonic variant which was cancelled as a result of Air Staff lack of interest in 1953 when the prototype was virtually complete. A principal factor affecting the P1083's cancellation was the Air Staff's preference for a larger unreheated engine, instead of the afterburning powerplant proposed for the P1083, and so the Hawker design team commenced work on a new mark of Hunter powered by an Avon 200 series turbojet developing 10,500lb st.

This page: WG131, a Hunter 6, was used for experimental tip-tank trials to improve performance without the drag that would result from underwing drop tanks. Unfortunately the idea was not successful and the experiment was abandoned. *(Top)* Side view of XG131 with tip-tanks and *(centre left and centre right)* close-ups of the wingtip installations. *(Above)* XG131 was put on static display at the 1956 Farnborough SBAC show after which the aircraft returned to service with No 14 Squadron. *BAe-Kingston*

The Hunter F6 prototype, bearing the Company designation P1099, employed the nose, centre fuselage and tail surfaces of the abandoned P1083 and building consequently progressed very rapidly, the aircraft — XF833 — making its first flight on 22 January 1954, 10 months ahead of the Mk 4. The prototype was delivered to the A&AEE at Boscombe Down for handling trials in February, but shortly afterwards it was damaged as a result of a forced landing following an engine failure. XF833 was repaired and flight trials were resumed, but the aircraft experienced a further engine failure and this time a full investigation revealed that the cause was compressor blade fatigue. Modifications were carried out to remedy the fault, but these resulted in the Avon 203 being de-rated from 10,500 to 10,000lb st. XF833 subsequently went on to complete handling, performance and gun firing trials at Hawkers and various Ministry establishments, and in 1956 it was delivered to Miles Aircraft Ltd for the installation of thrust reversal equipment under contract to Rolls-Royce.

Meanwhile, the first production Hunter F6, WW592, had flown on 25 March 1955, and this was followed by six more aircraft of the first batch, all of which — except WW597, which went to No 19 MU at RAF St Athan to give RAF technicians experience of the aircraft's systems — were used as trials aircraft. Perhaps the most interesting of this initial batch was WW594, which was designated P1109A and was completed as an aerodynamic test vehicle for the Firestreak air-to-air missile, being equipped with a large radome in a lengthened nose and carrying an

armament of only two guns. WW594 was never fitted with Firestreaks, but a later aircraft, XF378 (designated P1109B) carried full missile fire control equipment and had two Firestreaks fitted on underwing pylons. Operational Hunters were never equipped with the Firestreak, but both WW594 and XF378 contributed a great deal to the missile's development programme, the latter aircraft carrying out a number of successful test firings.

Hunter 6 production was undertaken at Kingston, Blackpool and Coventry, but the fighter's introduction into RAF service was delayed by a number of unexpected snags encountered during testing. Very early in the trials programme, it was found that the aircraft had a tendency to pitch up under high g loadings at high speed and high altitude, and considerable thought was given to ways of eradicating this unpleasant characteristic. In 1954, Hunter F1 WT568 was fitted with wing fences and put through an intensive series of high-altitude trials by the A&AEE; these did not provide the answer, but WT568 was then fitted with extended leading edges on the outer mainplanes and these were found to minimise the pitch-up tendency in tight turns by reducing the thickness/chord ratio of the outer wing sections and moving the aerodynamic centre of pressure forward. Extended leading edges subsequently became standard on all new production Hunters and were retrospectively fitted to a number of Mk 4s. High altitude gun firing was also found to produce a tendency to pitch down, but this was cured by the fitting of gun blast deflectors. In fact, a great deal of test work on gun firing at all altitudes was carried out with several early production Hunter 6s, notably XE543, XE558 and XE598, but few snags were encountered and the F6 was generally found to be a stable gun platform at all levels.

Large underwing tanks — 230gal — under test on XK161. Note also the bulge of the link collectors under the cockpit.
BAe-Kingston

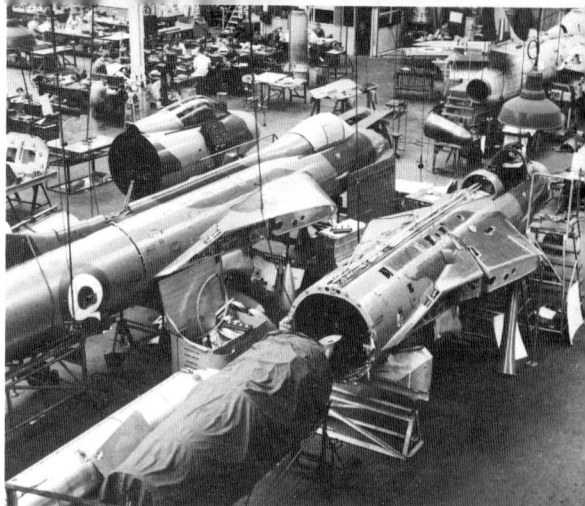

Top, left and right: Mk 6 Hunter production at Kingston, 1956. The aircraft nearest the camera, XE551, was retained by the A&AEE for miscellaneous trials. At the top right the stages in the T7 cockpit construction can be seen . *BAe-Kingston*

Left: Mk 6 XE588 was used for spinning trials by the A&AEE and afterwards went to Switzerland as a demonstration aircraft. This photograph gives an excellent view of the extensions to the wing leading-edges. *BAe-Kingston*

Top right: XK148, a Mk 6 seen here as an A&AEE trials aircraft equipped with RPs, was later sold to Chile as an FR71A. *BAe-Kingston*

Right: A rocket-armed Mk 6 shows its paces at Farnborough. *BAe-Kingston*

Although Hunter F6 production was well under way by the end of 1955, deliveries to Fighter Command squadrons did not begin until late the following year, mainly because RAF Maintenance Units, already overflowing with stocks of Hunter F4s, were unprepared to handle the new mark. The withdrawal of F4s from first-line squadrons and their replacement by F6s was consequently a slow process, but between October 1956 and the autumn of 1958, 18 RAF squadrons at home and in Germany had re-equipped with the latest Hunter variant. These were Nos, 1, 14, 19, 20, 26, 43, 54, 56, 63, 65, 66, 74, 92, 93, 111, 208, 247 and 263 Squadrons; a few F6s were

also supplied to No 4 Squadron just before its disbandment. No 208 Squadron's experience of the Hunter F6 was relatively short-lived; it took its aircraft to Cyprus in March 1958, but after only a year it re-equipped with de Havilland Venom FB4s, which it flew until receiving Hunter FGA9s in March 1960.

The Hunter F6 proved to he a highly popular aircraft in squadron service. Although its high speed performance offered no real advantage over that of the F4, because of airframe design limitations, the more powerful engine produced an increased rate of climb and the new automatic fuel system permitted the throttle to be banged open, closed and banged open

again without any risk of a flame out. Another feature of the F6s Avon 203 engine was the use of an isopropyl-nitrate starter instead of the cartridge starters used by earlier Hunters; this rotated the engine up to self-sustaining RPM much more quickly, permitting a faster scramble time.

Early production Hunter F6s, like previous variants, were fitted with a variable-incidence tailplane, the incidence of which could be varied by a button on the control column; later aircraft, however, had the more satisfactory arrangement of a 'flying tail' with a standard power-operated elevator and an electrical follow-up which altered the tailplane incidence in conjunction with elevator movement, improving longitudinal control at transonic speed.

By the time production of the Hunter F6 for the RAF ended in September 1957, 296 aircraft had been built at Kingston and a further 119 at Coventry by Armstrong-Whitworth Aircraft. It had been planned to produce a further 100 machines, but this part of the Ministry of Supply contract was cancelled following the appearance of the Duncan Sandys White Paper of 1957, which foresaw the replacement of manned interceptors by ground-to-air missiles in the early 1960s, and as a result Hawker Aircraft Ltd were compelled to close down their Blackpool factory and shift all production to Kingston. Fortunately, what might have turned out to be a black situation for the Company was restored by large orders for Mk 6 variants from India and Switzerland, followed by other overseas orders for refurbished aircraft (see Chapter 6).

By the middle of 1958 all RAF Hunter squadrons in Fighter Command and 2nd TAF had been equipped

with the Mk 6, and there were frequent squadron detachments to Malta and Cyprus. Although the type was to remain the standard home-based day fighter until the introduction of the supersonic English Electric Lightning in 1960, however, the Hunter 6 squadrons in Germany were gradually assuming a predominantly ground-attack role as the air defence task was assumed by USAF units equipped with supersonic types such as the F-100 Super Sabre and F-102A

Delta Dagger. For this reason, the Hawker design staff were preoccupied, from 1958-60, in modifying the aircraft to carry a still wider range of external stores, both of British and foreign origin. Also, the Suez operation of 1956 had turned the spotlight on the Hunter Mk 5s inadequate radius of action, and as a result much work was devoted to extending it by means of larger capacity drop tanks, designed as a private venture.

Above: A splendid view of Mk 6 XG129 with long-range tanks. It was Modification 223 which enabled the Hunter to carry four drop tanks on inner and outer pylons, although in practice few operational aircraft made use of the ability. *BAe-Kingston*

Left: Mk 6 XF442 with SNEB rocket pod experimentally mounted on outer wing pylons. *BAe-Kingston*

Top right: Hunter Mk 6s of No 92 Squadron over Yorkshire countryside in the 1950s. *MoD*

Bottom right: F6s of No 14 Squadron, 2nd TAF, over northern Germany in 1960. *MoD*

Top left: Winching up the Aden gun pack of an F6 of No 74 Squadron. In 1960, No 74 became the first RAF squadron to replace its Hunters with supersonic Lightning fighters. *MoD*

Top right: Replacing the ejection seat of a No 74 Squadron Hunter Mk 6. *MoD*

Above: Seen here in markings of No 79 Squadron with No 1 TWU, Mk 6 XK149 saw lengthy previous service with the Air Fighting Development Squadron. *RAF Official*

The new tanks could hold 230gal of fuel and were first tested, in dummy form, on Hunter Mk 4 WT798. Operationally, the tanks were carried on the inboard wing pylons of Avon 203-powered Hunters, and with two 100gal tanks carried on the outboard pylons this arrangement gave a total of 1,050gal. To demonstrate the feasibility of the new configuration, Hawkers' chief experimental test pilot, Hugh Merewether, flew Hunter 6 XF374 direct from Dunsfold to El Adem, in Libya, on 2 October 1958, covering the distance of 1,588 nautical miles in 3 hours 19 minutes. Despite the promise shown by the new tanks, however, it was not until late in 1959 that the Air Staff approved the necessary modifications to carry them, and these were incorporated in the FGA9 variant.

Hunter Aerobatic Teams

The Hunter was noted for its versatility as an aerobatic display aircraft. Best known of the Hunter display teams was 'Treble One' — No 111 Squadron, who flew in all-black aircraft — but many other teams thrilled aviation enthusiasts around the world and gained for the RAF a reputation that exists to this day and is furthered by the latest team, the Red Arrows.

Below: One of the most famous RAF aerobatic teams ever: the 'Black Arrows' of No 111 Squadron. *BAe-Kingston*

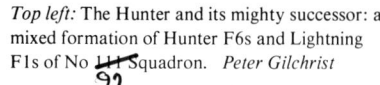

Top left: The Hunter and its mighty successor: a mixed formation of Hunter F6s and Lightning F1s of No ~~111~~ 92 Squadron. *Peter Gilchrist*

Above: No 92 Squadron's 'Blue Diamonds' over Cyprus. *MoD*

Left: 22 Hunters from Nos 111 and 43 Squadrons at the 1958 SBAC Show. *MoD*

Top right: Mk 6s of No 92 Squadron's team, the precursors of the 'Blue Diamonds', at Linton-on-Ouse in the late 1950s. *MoD*

Centre right: Another view of the 'Blue Diamonds', here taking off from RAF Akrotiri, Cyprus. *MoD*

Bottom right: XL571 in the neat royal blue paintwork of the 'Blue Diamonds', No 92 Squadron's aerobatic team at RAF Middleton-St-George in the late 1950s. *Peter Gilchrist*

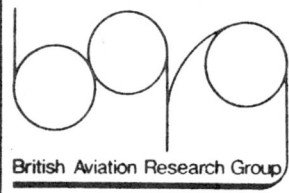

INTERNATIONAL AIR TATTOO 79
GREENHAM COMMON
a check-list of participating and visiting aircraft

British Aviation Research Group

PREPARED FOR ENTHUSIASTS BY ENTHUSIASTS

PRICE 15p   THIS LIST CORRECT TO 6.00pm ON FRIDAY 22nd JUNE 1979

Lockheed Hercules 25th anniversary line-up:

TC-67	C-130H	Argentine AF/1 Brigada Aerea
A97-008	C-130H	Royal Australian AF/36 Sqdn
2454	C-130E	Brazilian AF/1º/1º GT
130316	C-130E	Canadian AF/435 Sqdn
B-678	C-130H	Royal Danish AF/Esk721
436/4X-FBW	C-130H	Israeli DF/AF
NZ7001	C-130H	Royal New Zealand AF/40 Sqdn
955/UN	C-130H	Royal Norwegian AF/335 Skv
6805	C-130H	Portuguese AF/Esc 501
1619	C-130H	Royal Saudi AF/16 Sqdn
TK10-7/301-07	KC-130H	Spanish AF/312 Esc
XV200	Hercules C.1	RAF/Lyneham Tactical Wing
XV302	Hercules C.1	RAF/Lyneham Tactical Wing
XV208	Hercules W.2	RAE Farnborough/Met. Research Flight
41640	C-130A	USAF/Tennessee ANG (105thTAS)
50023	C-130A	USAF/AFRes (928thTAG) "City of Ardmore"
70493	C-130D	USAF/New York ANG (139thTAS)
37876	C-130E	USAF/No badge
10941	C-130E	USAF/39thTAS
96566	C-130E	USAF/435thTAW
149797/JM-797	C-130F	US Navy/VR-24
1602/5	HC-130H	US Coast Guard/Kodiak
95827	HC-130N	USAF/67thARRS
60220	HC-130P	USAF/67thARRS
4224	C-130H	Venezuelan AF

US Army detachment

74-22283	CH-47C	295th Aviation Company
74-22286	"	"
76-22677	"	"
67-19491	UH-1H	503rd Aviation Company
71-20162	"	"
73-21752	"	"
68-16765	OH-58A	"
68-16963	"	" (left for Germany 22.6)
69-16137	"	"
69-16200	"	"
71-20538	"	"
72-21214	"	"
72-21217	"	"
72-21399	"	"
67-15560	AH-1S	"
67-15640	"	"
68-15011	"	"
68-15086	"	"
70-15975	"	"
70-15982	"	"

70-16017	AH-1S	503rd Aviation Company
70-16024	"	"
70-16029	"	"
70-16056	"	"
70-16076	"	"
70-16089	"	" (left for Germany 22.6)
70-16093	"	"
71-21020	"	"
71-21024	"	"
71-21038	"	"

Aircraft on static display (North side):

BA10	Mirage 5BA	Belgian AF/3 Wing
FT28	T-33A	" 11 Esc
FT29	"	" 11 Esc
CF05	Merlin IIIA	" 15 Wing
10735	CP107 Argus	Canadian AF/415 Sqdn
104760	CF-104	" Sollingen Wing
AT-157	SK35XD Draken	Royal Danish AF/Esk725
556/4-BB	Mirage IIIE	French AF/EC-4
76	Nord 262D	French AF/ET-65 (moved to south side)
42	Atlantic	Aeronavale
20+01	F-104G	W.German AF/JbG-31
20+02	"	" JbG-32
32+80	G-91R	" WS-50
35+03	RF-4E	" AkG-51
35+07	"	" AkG-51
MM40122/30-07	Atlantic	Italian AF/30° Stormo
D-8051	F-104G	Royal Netherlands AF/Volkel Wing
K-4016	NF-5B	" 313 Sqdn
209/V	SP-2H Neptune	Royal Netherlands Navy/320 Sqdn
263/K	UH-14A Lynx	" 7 Sqdn
PH-NLH	Hunter T.7	Fokker NV
890	CF-104	Royal Norwegian AF/334 Skv
4633	CF-104D	" 334 Skv
C12-40	F-4C	Spanish AF/Ala12 (ex-USAF 40896)
J-1704	Venom FB.54	Swiss AF (for RAF Museum)
80217	C-5A	USAF/436thMAW
60152	C-141A	" 437thMAW
80258	B-52G	" 416thBW
37990	KC-135A	" 305thARW
10880	C-9A	" 435thTAW
24461	CT-39A	" 58thMAS
24198	VC-140B	" 58thMAS
31213	C-12A	" 58thMAS
14630	OV-10A	" 601stTCW
80392/HR white	F-4E	" 50thTFW
80568/AR blue	RF-4C	" 10thTRW
01551/51	F-5E	" 10thTRW
80054/UH red	F-111E	" 20thTFW
70231/WR	A-10A	" 81stTFW
70158/CR orange	F-15B	" 32ndTFS
95785	HH-53C	" 67thARRS
72+29	UH-1D	W.German Army
N64	Sabreliner	FAA Frankfurt
159441/AG-110	F-14A	US Navy/VF-143 (USS Eisenhower)
159584/AG-602	EA-6B	" VAQ-138 "
160418/AG-013	E-2C	" VAW-121 "
160564/AG-301	A-7E	" VA-66 "
153437/LE-4	P-3B	" VP-11
141023	C-131F	" Mildenhall
M-071	Alouette III	Danish AF/Esk 722
1233	Canberra B.82	Venezuelan AF.

XV262/62	Nimrod MR.1	St.Mawgan Wing
WR965/65	Shackleton AEW.2	8 Sqdn
XT275/A	Buccaneer S.2B	15 Sqdn
XZ395	Jaguar GR.1	54 Sqdn
XR724	Lightning F.6	RAF Binbrook (joint 5 & 11 Sqdn marks)
XV424	Phantom FGR.2	56 Sqdn (Alcock & Brown markings)
XV501/O	"	29 Sqdn
XJ784	Vulcan B.2	44 Sqdn
XL231	Victor K.2	57 Sqdn
XH167	Canberra PR.9	39 Sqdn
XZ445/Q	Harrier T.4	2330CU
XS738/U	Dominie T.1	6FTS
XX499/G	Jetstream T.1	6FTS
XF445/Q	Hunter FGA.9	2TWU
XL619/06	Hunter T.7	2TWU
XX265/140	Hawk T.1	1TWU/234 Sqdn
XS641	Andover C.1	115 Sqdn
XX553/07	Bulldog T.1	London UAS
XW902/H	Ga elle HT.3	CFS (H)
XP359	Whirlwind HAR.10	RAF recruiting display
'XX824'	Jaguar GR.1 replica	RAF recruiting display
KF183/3	Harvard T.2B	A&AEE
XS765	Basset CC.1	A&AEE
XX919	BAC 1-11	RAE Farnborough
XJ608	Sea Vixen FAW.2	RAE Bedford "Chalkie"
WH774	Canberra PR.7	RAE Bedford
WK163	Canberra B.6	RAE Bedford
XP820	Beaver AL.1	AAC Centre
XR244	Auster AOP.9	AAC Centre
WP964	Chipmunk T.10	AAC Centre
LB312	Taylorcraft	AAC Centre
XT624	Scout AH.1	AAC Centre
XT131/B	Sioux AH.1	AAC Centre
G-SCUB/542447	Piper Cub	Private
G-BDAM/216	Harvard	Private
G-BGEV	Piper Tomahawk	Private
G-BFTO	Rotorway Scorpion	Private

Aircraft taking part in flying programme or visiting (South side):

422/B	SAAB 1050E	Austrian AF/Karo As
423/C	"	" Karo As
427/G	"	" Karo As
428/H	"	" Karo As
429/I	"	" Karo As
402/B	"	" Yellow Sqdn
T-430	SAAB Supporter	Royal Danish AF
H-207	Hughes 500	"
603/4-BI	Mirage IIIE	French AF/EC-4
21+18	F-104G	W.German Navy/MFG-2
21+27	"	" MFG-2
50+62	Transall	W.German AF/LTG-61
84+38	CH-53G	W.German Army
61+16	Atlantic	W.German Navy/MFG-3
C-10	F-27M Troopship	R.Netherlands AF/334 Sqdn
K-3020	NF-5A	" 313 Sqdn
K-3028	"	" 313 Sqdn
131	F-5A	R.Norwegian AF/338 Skv
574	"	" 338 Skv
2406	T-37C	Portuguese AF/Asas de Portugal
2414	"	" Asas de Portugal
2415	"	" Asas de Portugal
2423	"	" Asas de Portugal

Registration	Type	Operator
2426	T-37C	Portuguese AF/Asas de Portugal
2429	"	" Asas de Portugal
2430	"	" Asas de Portugal
T12B-13/745-13	CASA C212	Spanish AF/Esc 745
A-713	Twin Bonanza	Swiss AF
J-4022	Hunter F.58	Swiss AF/Patrouille Suisse
J-4025	"	" Patrouille Suisse
J-4026	"	" Patrouille Suisse
J-4027	"	" Patrouille Suisse
J-4028	"	" Patrouille Suisse
J-4030	"	" Patrouille Suisse
70081/CR orange	F-15A	USAF/32ndTFS
70234/WR	A-10A	" 81stTFW
14684	OV-10A	" 601stTCW
01560/60	F-5E	" 10thTRW
G-AKKB	Gemini	Private
G-ASSS	Cessna 172	" (hangared)
G-ATBG	Nord 1002	"
JY-AFK	Piper Seneca	Jordanian Falcons display team
JY-RJG	Pitts Special	"
JY-RJH	"	"
G-BBOH	"	Marlborough display team
G-BDXZ	"	"
OE-FPK	Piper Twin Comanche	Private ('Karo As' support)
XV185	Hercules	Lyneham Tactical Wing
XX764/13	Jaguar GR.1	2260CU
XX766/14	"	"
XV488/R	Phantom FGR.2	2280CU
XV438/Y	"	"
XP749/A	Lightning F.3	Lightning Training Flight
XP764/B	"	"
XV354	Buccaneer S.2	2370CU
XV357	"	"
WR963/63	Shackleton AEW.2	8 Sqdn
XV748/B	Harrier GR.3	2330CU
XV760/F	"	"
XM605	Vulcan B.2	50 Sqdn
WJ817	Canberra PR.7	13 Sqdn
XZ588	Sea King HAR.3	RAF Sea King Training Unit
XX230/129	Hawk T.1	1TWU/63 Sqdn
XX280/142	"	"
XW352/R	Jet Provost T.5B	6FTS
XW309/V	"	"
XX524/04	Bulldog T.1	London UAS
WF791	Meteor T.7	CFS Vintage Pair
XH304	Vampire T.11	"
XW884 'CU/41'	Gazelle HT.2	705 Sqdn 'Sharks'
XW863 'CU/42'	"	"
XX397 'CU/43'	"	"
XW891 'CU/49'	"	"
XW894 'CU/52'	"	"
TF956 'T/123'	Sea Fury FB.11	RN Historic Aircraft Flight
LS326 '5A'	Swordfish	"
XZ232 'BM/333'	Lynx HAS.2	702 Sqdn (HMS Birmingham Flight)
WT804 'VL/831'	Hunter GA.11	FRADU 'Blue Herons'
XE682 '835'	"	"
WV267 '836'	"	"
WT806 '838'	"	"
XF977 '865'	"	"
XZ203	Lynx AH.1	AAC Centre
XZ341	Gazelle AH.1	"

(Note: A few additional arrivals are expected for the show on Saturday/Sunday)

3
The Hunter
Two-Seaters

Hunter T Mk 7

Hawker Aircraft Ltd's proposal to develop a two-seat version of the Hunter to replace the Meteor T7 and Vampire T11 in service with the Royal Air Force's operational conversion units, advanced flying schools, instrument training schools and weapons schools dates back to 1953, when the Company's project team evolved two possible configurations, one based on a tandem and the other on a side-by-side seating arrangement. Although tandem seating appeared at first sight to be the more logical, since it fitted in more appropriately with the aerodynamic characteristics of the Hunter airframe, discussions with RAF instructors at the Central Flying School and the Central Fighter Establishment gradually led to the adoption of the side-by-side arrangement, this being more acceptable from the instructional point of view.

Under the Company designation P1101, Hawker Aircraft initiated the Hunter trainer programme as a private venture and a mock-up was constructed. This at first featured a 'double bulge' canopy, but this was smoothed out and the canopy design now incorporated two large transparent panels set in a single big frame, electrically-operated to open upwards and backwards. It was also decided to incorporate an armament of two Aden guns semi-buried in blisters on either side of the fuselage nose beneath the cockpit.

In 1954, Specification T157D was written around the Hawker design and work went ahead on the building of a prototype, XJ615, at Kingston. This aircraft was based on the Hunter F Mk 4 and was powered by a Rolls-Royce Avon RA21 engine rated at 7,500lb st.

It flew for the first time on 8 July 1955 and, painted pale green overall, took part in the SBAC display at Farnborough the following September. XJ615 originally carried the two-gun armament, but the port gun was later removed.

Early flight trials with the P1101 prototype revealed serious problems created by the canopy design and the enlarged fuselage cross-section. At speeds of over 0.84M, the airflow around the hood and hood fairing became rapidly more unstable until, at 0.88M, the airflow noise level became virtually intolerable and the aircraft began snaking and pitching. A. W. 'Bill' Bedford, who took over from Neville Duke as Chief Test Pilot in 1956, reported that: 'Flying at high speed in the T7 in those days, the pilot heard a noise like an express train racing through a tunnel. Looking through the side of the canopy, he could see the hazy blue shock waves building up and moving back as the Mach number increased. Before long the entire rear portion of the canopy would be surrounded by a halo of shock waves. Very picturesque, but the associated noise and buffet level was unacceptable and most uncomfortable for the pilot. It also made a great drag on performance.'

One of the principal figures involved in isolating the trouble was Mr H. J. Rochfort, the head of the Research and Development Section at Hawkers, who flew on many occasions with Bedford and other pilots to measure the pressure distribution over the canopy. From his own first-hand observations he suggested that the probable solution was to modify the rear decking of the cockpit canopy; this was done by degrees, over 20 different fairing configurations being tested, until in the middle of 1956 the whole fairing was raised, contoured and area-ruled, giving the two-seat Hunter its characteristic hump-backed appearance.

Meanwhile, Hawkers had been authorised to build a second P1101 prototype, XJ627, powered by a Rolls-Royce Avon 203 engine. This flew in 1956 and, since its 10,000lb st engine was the same as that installed in the Hunter F6, it was expected that the second aircraft would form the basis of future RAF and overseas orders. Instead, the emphasis remained on the further

Below left: XJ615, the prototype T7 two-seater; note interim fairing aft of the cockpit. *BAe-Kingston*

Top: XJ615 showing two-gun armament and panels over the canopy during the trials of the fairing behind the cockpit. This aircraft was written off on 26 June 1964. *BAe-Kingston*

Above and right: XL574, the T7 used for spinning trials at the Empire Test Pilot's School. Note nose probe and various anti-spin devices on the tail, detailed *(right)*. *BAe-Kingston*

development and refinement of the lower-powered first prototype, XJ615, which in 1956 was fitted with a brake parachute.

Structurally, the Hunter two-seater was identical to the single-seat F4 aft of the front transport joint, fully duplicated flying controls and gunsights being provided for instructor and pupil. Once the high-speed instability problems had been sorted out, performance was similar in all respects to that of the Hunter F4 — evidenced by the fact that Mk 4 aerobatic teams were often led by a two-seater. The principal difference was that the new two-seat nose increased the overall length by 3in to 48ft 10.5in, and the clean all-up weight to 17,200lb.

The original contract called for the production of 55 Hunter T Mk 7s for the Royal Air Force, but 10 of these were subsequently allocated to the Royal Navy as T Mk 8s (qv). Production was scheduled to be undertaken at Blackpool, but following the cancellation of part of the Hunter 6 order, it was moved to Kingston. This caused only a slight delay and the first production T7, XL563, flew on 11 October 1957,

deliveries being made to No 229 Operational Conversion Unit at RAF Chivenor, Devon, in mid-1958. Many of the 45 T7s built for the RAF were in fact delivered to 229 OCU, but most operational Hunter squadrons at home and overseas had one trainer on their inventory and other examples werc delivered to No 4 FTS at Valley, No 402 Weapons Training Unit on Stylt and to various station flights (see Appendix 1). Some T7s were also eventually allocated to Jaguar, Phantom and Buccaneer OCUs.

In its early Service career the Hunter T Mk 7 experienced some spinning problems, and XL570 crashed as the result of an inverted spin on 29 August 1958. T Mk 7 XL574 was subsequently allocated to the Empire Test Pilots' School to carry out a lengthy series of spinning trials, for which purpose it was fitted with a nose cone carrying pivoting cones to measure angle of attack and yaw and also an anti-spin parachute mounted in a housing above the tailpipe, together with telemetry equipment. About 1,200 spins were carried out, and it was found that spin recovery presented no problems provided the appropriate recovery action was initiated in time — in other words, within a maximum of two turns. The same applied to all other marks of Hunter, although intentional inverted spinning remained prohibited. However, Hawker's confidence in the ability of the T7 to recover from a spin satisfactorily was ably demonstrated by Bill Bedford at Farnborough in 1959 and 1960, when he held the aircraft in for 12 full turns before recovering.

As well as the 45 T7s newly-built for the RAF, several Mk 4s were also converted to T7 standard (see Appendix 1). One of these aircraft was XF310, which had previously been used for the Fireflash AAM trials. Twenty T7s were still in service with either the RAF or Ministry establishments at the end of 1980.

Above left: Nose view of a T7 of No 4 FTS, RAF Valley, showing the special gun blast deflector for the T7. *MoD*

Left and top right: Two views of XL591 in natural finish and then in the resplendent red and white used by the RAF's Air Fighting Development Squadron. *Peter Gilchrist*

Left: T7s of No 237 OCU; in the foreground T7A XL614. *MoD*

Below left: XL577, a T7 from 229 OCU, RAF Chivenor, on approaches to Biggin Hill on 19 September 1969. *Dennis Robinson*

Below: Hunter T8M XL602 used by the RAE for development work in connection with the Harrier's 'Blue Fox' radar. *Peter Gilchrist*

Hunter T Mk 8

Ten of the original 55 T7s destined for the RAF were in the event completed as T Mk 8s for the Royal Navy, and a prototype aircraft — originally Mk 4 WW664, which had been repaired following an accident and then converted — flew for the first time on 3 March 1958, followed by the first newly-built aircraft, XL580, on 30 May. Seventeen more Mk 4s were subsequently converted to T8 standard and were allocated to the Fleet Air Arm's 738, 759 and 764 Squadrons at Yeovilton and Lossiemouth. The Hunter T8 differed from its RAF counterpart by the provision of naval radio equipment and an airfield emergency arrester hook; later, aircraft were modified to carry 2in rocket batteries and Bullpup missiles. During the 1960s, further Mk 4 airframes were converted to T8B and T8C standard, fitted with OR946 instrument dis-

plays and TACAN equipment; gunsights, guns and nose radomes were deleted from these machines. Some RAF T7s were also equipped to a similar standard under the designation T7A. Several T8s were still in service with the the Royal Navy in 1980, and one example — XL602 — was used by the Royal Aircraft Establishment in the development of Blue Fox radar for the Sea Harrier, this particular Hunter bearing the designation T8M.

Top: WW664, converted in 1957 to become a prototype T8 for the Royal Navy. *BAe-Kingston*

Above: XL580, an immaculate T8 of the Navy's No 764 Squadron. *BAe-Kingston*

Hunter Mk 12

The Hunter 12, powered by an Avon 203 engine, was a converted Mk 6, XE531, which was ordered by the Ministry of Supply for RAE trials with various avionics associated with the ill-fated TSR2. It was fitted with a nose-mounted vertical survey camera and a head-up display, and the original intention was for this aircraft to be the forerunner of a small batch of Mk 12s which were to be used in the training of TSR2 crews. With the cancellation of TSR2 in 1965, the sole Mk 12 was used by RAE Farnborough and RAE Bedford in development work associated with instrumentation for the Hawker Siddeley Harrier. The Mk 12 carried no armament and was finished in a high-gloss green and white paint scheme.

G-APUX

From 1959, following a slow start, overseas sales of Hunter trainers began to gather impetus and involved both Mk 4 and Mk 6 conversions. In the Company's bid to sell converted Mk 6s (mostly aircraft returned by overseas air forces) a great deal of valuable work was done by a company-sponsored demonstration aircraft, G-APUX, which was built in the summer of 1959 using the wings and rear fuselage of a former Belgian Air Force Hunter 6, IF-19, and a front fuselage section which had been on display at the Paris Air Show in June that year. Fitted with a larger diameter brake parachute than other Hunters, G-APUX was the aircraft used by Bill Bedford to demonstrate prolonged spinning at Farnborough in 1959 and 1960. It was demonstrated in Switzerland and the Middle East, and was flown with 350-gallon long-range ferry tanks. In 1963-65 it was used for a time by the Iraqi, Jordanian and Lebanese air forces before being returned to Britain and eventually delivered to Chile as a Mk 72 in 1967.

Details of G-APUX's career overseas, and of the Hunter T7 export variants, will be found in Chapter 6.

Above: Mk 12 XE531; finished in high-gloss green and white paint scheme, this aircraft was used to test avionics associated with the ill-fated TSR2. *BAe-Kingston*

Right: Another view of XE531, the sole Mk 12, with long-range tanks. Had the TSR2 entered production, more Mk 12s would have been produced for conversion training. This nose detail shows the bulges that housed terrain-following radar equipment destined for TSR2. *BAe-Kingston*

Below right: G-APUX, Hawker Siddeley's renowned two-seat Hunter demonstrator. The aircraft was finally delivered to Chile in 1967, changing designation from Mk 66A to Mk 72. *Peter Gilchrist*

No 20 Squadron in Malaya

A former RAF Germany Hunter Mk 6 squadron, No 20 was revived at Tengah, Singapore, in September 1961, equipped with FGA9s. Its role was ground attack, and its service in the Far East included the period of confrontation with Indonesia from 1963 to 1966, when the squadron's Hunters carried out rocket attacks on groups of suspected Indonesian terrorists believed to have been parachuted into the swamps of Johore, on the southern tip of the Malay Peninsula.

During these operations, No 20 was unique among RAF Hunter FGA squadrons in that it operated a flight of Pioneer CC1 aircraft in the forward air control role.

During its time in South-East Asia, No 20 Squadron also took part in regular exercises and deployments to other SEATO countries, and in 1962 it spent six months in Thailand. The Squadron disbanded at Tengah on 18 February 1970 and later became a Jaguar squadron at RAF Bruggen, in Germany.

Top left: Hunter FGA9 carrying RPs over the Malaysian coast during the Indonesian 'confrontation'. *MoD*

Bottom left: XL619, a T7, landing at Tengah, 1968. *Brian Lawrence*

Above: Hunter Mk 6 over Borneo, 1969. XJ685 was converted to become an FGA9. *Brian Lawrence*

Below: Hunter FGA9 landing at Tengah, 1968. *Brian Lawrence*

More views of No 20 Squadron Hunters from Tengah, Singapore
1968. *Brian Lawrence*

Below: FGA9s on the flight line at Tengah. *MoD*

4
Last of the Breed

Above: FGA9s on detachment to Gibraltar during a NATO exercise. *Peter Gilchrist*

Hunter FGA9

The last fighter/ground attack variant of the Hunter to serve with the Royal Air Force, the FGA9, owed its origin to an urgent requirement for a more modern aircraft to replace the ageing de Havilland Venom in the Middle East from 1960 onwards. In 1958, therefore, Hawker Aircraft Ltd received an order to convert the first of 100 Hunter F6s to a new tropical standard under the designation FGA9, the majority to be powered by Rolls-Royce Avon 207 engines of 10,050lb st and to have a greatly increased underwing stores capacity as well as a greater endurance.

While Hawker's Kingston factories were engaged in converting full-standard Mk 9s, a number of Mk 6 airframes were modified by RAF maintenance units to carry 230gal drop tanks; these aircraft were known as the Mk 6/Interim Mk 9, and relatively few were delivered. Full-standard Mk 9s were all converted from Mk 6 airframes, the prototype aircraft — XG135 — flying on 3 July 1959. The FGA9 was completely tropicalised, with more adequate cockpit ventilation and increased oxygen supply for the pilot to permit long-range operations. Because of the condition and small size of most airfields in the Middle East, the FGA9 was also fitted with a brake parachute of 13ft 6in diameter.

Like all single-seat Hunter variants, the FGA9 carried a built-in armament of four 30mm Aden guns in their detachable pack. However, it was the variety of underwing stores that could be carried which made the FGA9 a truly formidable ground attack aircraft — and one which, moreover, gave an enormous boost to the RAF's ability to carry out rapid reinforcement of overseas theatres from bases in the United Kingdom. On the inboard pylons of the specially strengthened wing, the aircraft could carry two 1,000lb bombs, two 500lb bombs, two practice bomb carriers each holding a pair of 25lb practice bombs, two clusters of six 3in rockets, two 2in rocket batteries each containing either 24 or 37 folding-fin rockets, two 100gal phenolic asbestos drop tanks or two 230gal Hawker mild steel drop tanks, to accommodate which latter the FGA9 was fitted with cutaway flaps; while on the outboard pylons there was provision for two 100gal drop tanks or up to

24 3in No 1 Mk 5 rocket projectiles on standard Mk 12 rocket rails. The 100gal drop tanks could also be used as napalm bombs.

The Hunter FGA9 entered service with No 8 Squadron at Khormaksar, Aden, in January 1960, and later in the year No 208 Squadron at Nairobi and No 43 at Leuchars, in Scotland, also re-equipped with the new variant. Both these units eventually joined No 8 at Khormaksar and all three were to render invaluable service in security operations against dissident tribes in Aden and the Arabian Gulf states; a full account of their activities will be found in Chapter 9.

Two other overseas RAF squadrons were equipped with the Hunter FGA9. The first of these was No 20, which, having been disbanded as a Hunter F6 unit at Gutersloh in 1960, was revived at Tengah, Singapore, in September 1961, equipped with FGA9s which had been ferried out from the United Kingdom. Its role was ground attack and its service in South-East Asia included the period of Indonesian 'confrontation' from December 1963 to August 1966. During 1962-63 No 20 Squadron was involved in SEATO (South-East Asia Treaty Organisation) exercises and deployments, and in October 1963 it was deployed to Labuan and Kuching for the first time. This detachment to the East Malaysian (North Borneo) territories was to be a familiar one for the squadron during the confrontation

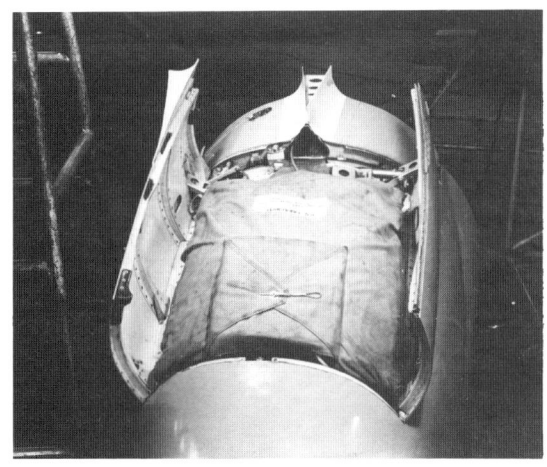

Above: Detail of brake parachute stowage in the FGA9. *BAe-Kingston*

Below: Hunter FGA9s of No 1 TWU in the markings of Nos 79, 63 and 264 'Shadow Squadrons'. *MoD*

Bottom: Mk 9 of No 1 TWU, Brawdy streams its landing parachute. *RAF Official*

period. When the latter ended in August 1966 the practice of sending off four-aircraft detachments came to an end and the Squadron entered into a routine of training and exercises, with occasional deployments. At the height of the confrontation, when groups of Indonesian terrorists were parachuted into Malaysian territory, the squadron's Hunters carried out rocket attacks on groups of suspected hostile troops in the inaccessible swamps of Johore, on the southern end of the Malay Peninsula. In 1962, before the confrontation, the squadron had spent six months on detachment in Thailand as part of a SEATO strike force during the Laotian crisis.

An unusual feature of No 20 Squadron's career was that, for the last year of its life as a Hunter squadron from January to December 1969, it operated a flight of Pioneer CC1 aircraft in the forward air control role. The squadron disbanded at Tengah on 18 February 1970 and later became a Jaguar Squadron at Bruggen, in RAF Germany.

The other overseas FGA9 squadron was No 28, which was based at Kai Tak, Hong Kong, from June 1962, being fully equipped by 28 August when the last of its Hunters arrived from the UK. It had previously operated Venom FB4s. During its $4\frac{1}{2}$ years of operations in Hong Kong with Hunters it took part in Army and Navy co-operation exercises, firepower demonstrations, practice interceptions, long-range training and liaison flights, detachments to East Malaysia (Borneo), border reconnaissance and practice diversions to Sek Kong airfield. The main problems it encountered operationally were climatic — typhoons, dense fogs and torrential rain.

A ceremonial parade to mark 28 Squadron's disbandment was held at Kai Tak on 15 December 1966 and the unit's two remaining Hunters (the rest having been returned to the UK) made their last landing there on 23 December. The squadron later re-equipped with Wessex HC2 helicopters and in 1981 was operating these from Sek Kong as the only RAF flying unit permanently based in the Far East.

At home, meanwhile, two first-line squadrons operated Hunter FGA9s during the 1960s; these were Nos 1 and 54, which were based at Stradishall, Waterbeach and West Raynham and which provided the offensive element of No 38 Group, the tactical force of RAF Air Support Command. The Hunters of these two squadrons continued to play a useful operational role until 1969, standing ready to fly to any trouble spot in the Near, Middle or Far East to bolster forces already in situ, and they took part in frequent exercises involving rapid reinforcement of the various NATO commands. In October 1969 No 1 Squadron re-formed at Wittering with V/STOL Harriers, and No 54 re-equipped with Phantoms the following year. The Hunter FGA9s continued to operate alongside both these new types for some time, but were eventually phased out of first-line service and either repurchased by Hawker Siddeley or allocated to training units.

By the end of 1970 about 50 Hunter FGA Mk 9s remained in RAF service, but their useful life was far from over. On 1 August 1972 No 45 Squadron was re-formed with Hunter FGA9s (and one T7) at West Raynham, moving to Wittering in September, and on 1 August 1973 No 58 Squadron was also formed at Wittering with the same type of aircraft. The Hunter Wing formed by these two units was intended to provide a pool of experience in ground attack techniques for pilots destined to join the RAF's Jaguar and other front-line squadrons. On 26 July 1976, with the build-up of these new squadrons virtually complete, the Hunter Wing at Wittering was disbanded. Its task was taken over by the Tactical Weapons Unit, which was formed in September 1974 at RAF Brawdy on the coast of Pembrokeshire to provide a tactical stepping-stone between No 4 Advanced Flying Training School at Valley and the Phantom, Jaguar and Harrier OCUs.

Most of the TWU's Hunters came from the long-serving Hunter OCU, No 229, which had now been disbanded, and were a mixture of F6s, FGA9s and F6As, the latter featuring a strengthened Mk 9-type wing and a brake parachute. There were also, of course, the ubiquitous T7 trainers.

The TWU consisted of three 'shadow' squadrons, Nos 79, 63 and 234. No 79 Squadron's task was to give a short course to refresh pilots who had come from ground jobs or who were to be weapons instructors, while the function of the other two squadrons was to provide a long course of $4\frac{1}{2}$ months — involving 60 hours' flying — designed to give pilots fresh from the FTS at Valley sufficient tactical experience to convert to a front-line unit with minimum delay. The first step was a familiarisation flight in a Hunter T7, which was followed by formation flying, gunsight-handling excercises and dogfighting techniques, leading up to live ground-attack training including cannon firing, sorties with SNEB rockets and dive-bombing. The course concentrated on typical operational profiles, with low-level sorties flown against selected targets in designated low-flying areas, and considerable emphasis was placed on navigational skills. Some TWU Hunters were allocated a secondary

Facing page: FGA9 of No 54 Squadron, No 38 Group at RAF Stradishall in the 1960s, showing the cartridge case chute over the link collector. *MoD*

Left: FGA9 of No 54 Squadron on detachment in Norway on Exercise 'Winter Express'. *MoD*

Below: Changing the weapons pack of a Hunter FGA9 of No 28 Squadron, RAF Kai Tak, Hong Kong. *MoD*

Above: FGA9 serving with No 233 (Harrier) OCU, RAF Wittering. *Peter Gilchrist*

Facing page: One of the famous 'Blue Diamonds' — No 92 Squadron's aerobatic team.The aircraft is an F6. *BAe Kingston*

air defence role, and as late as 1980, during NATO's Exercise 'Crusader', were deployed in that capacity for the point defence in industrial installations in various parts of the United Kingdom. The TWU also maintained a detached flight of Hunters on Gibraltar, with the secondary task of providing fast reconnassiance of the western Mediterranean.

The decision to concentrate the Tactical Weapons Unit at Brawdy was partly a political one, aimed at creating more jobs in an area of high unemployment, but it was found that a lot of flying hours were being lost through bad weather and as a consequence the unit could not meet the RAF's increased demand for pilots. In September 1978 30 Hunters were therefore transferred to Lossiemouth, in Scotland, to form No 2 Tactical Weapons Unit, and this had the added benefit of relieving congestion at Brawdy as the TWU there began to receive the BAe Hawk, the first of which was delivered in December 1977.

No 2 TWU moved from Lossiemouth to Chivenor in 1980, when the latter base was reactivated, and also equipped with Hawks, its Hunters returning to Brawdy for service with No 1 TWU. At the end of 1980 No 1 TWU had a complement of 46 Hawk T1s, 19 single-seat Hunters of various marks (concentrated in No 79 Squadron), six two-seat Hunters, a few Jet Provosts and two Meteors for target-towing duties. The last Hunter instructors' course was completed in May 1979, but the graceful lines of the Hawker fighter will remain a familiar sight in Welsh skies for some time to come.

Hunter FR Mk 10

The feasibility of mounting nose cameras in the Hunter for fast fighter-reconnaissance work was first tested by Hawker Aircraft Ltd on an early production Mk 4, WT780, and in 1958 the Company received a Ministry of Supply contract for the conversion of a number of Mk 6s to carry three nose-mounted cameras, the aircraft being destined for service with the RAF in Germany in the short-range reconnaissance role. Forty aircraft were so converted over a

Right: Nose view of the camera installation in an FR Mk 10. *BAe-Kingston*

Below right: FR10 XG168 seen with long-range tanks. One of the third batch of Kingston-built Mk 6s, XG168 served with No 79 Squadron. *BAe-Kingston*

three-year period, beginning with the prototype, XF429, which flew on 7 November 1959, and the majority were delivered to Nos 2 and 4 Squadrons in Germany, replacing the Swift FR5. The role of both squadrons was primarily visual reconnaissance at very low level, the aircraft being controlled by a NATO-administered Tactical Operations Centre, and could be called upon to operate anywhere within the NATO area from northern Norway to Greece. Fighter-recce pilots found the Hunter FR10 a near-ideal mount for its task, being able to operate at 620kts at zero feet and possessing sufficient range, with 230gal drop tanks, to fly from Germany to Malta non-stop. Its armament of four 30mm cannon, too, would have enabled it to fight its way out of trouble or to slow down most moving ground targets until ground attack support could be called up. Both 2 and 4 Squadrons scored repeated successes in the short-range section of Royal Flush, the annual NATO photo-reconnaissance competition, the Hunter being considerably more flexible and manoeuvrable than other NATO FR types such as the RF-101 Voodoo. Each FR Hunter squadron had its own team of Army Ground Liaison Officers and worked in co-ordination with a Mobile Field Photographic Unit, whose task was to process and interpret the film brought back by the aircraft. Both squadrons operated Hunter FR10s until the late 1960s, when No 2 Squadron became a Jaguar tactical reconnaissance unit and No 4 eventually received V/STOL Harriers.

Small numbers of fighter-reconnaissance Hunters were sold to overseas air forces (see Chapter 6).

Hunter GA11

In 1960-62, a conversion order was placed by the Ministry of Supply on behalf of the Admiralty for a batch of ex-RAF Hunter Mk 4s to be modified for the training role in the Fleet Air Arm by the removal of the cannon armament, the fitting of an airfield arrester hook under the rear fuselage and provision for rocket launchers on underwing pylons. Forty aircraft were converted under the designation GA Mk 11; a few were also fitted with nose cameras and designated PR Mk 11A. The naval Hunters were operated by various weapon training establishments, mainly the Fleet Requirements and Aircraft Direction Unit at RNAS Yeovilton, in Somerset, from which base they were within easy reach of the main RN fleet establishments at Portsmouth and Portland. The Hunters were operated under contract by Airwork Services Ltd and were used for dummy attacks (both solo and multi-aircraft) on Fleet units, as well as for radar calibration tasks. Each GA11 (and some two-seat T8Cs) carried a Harley light in the nose for visual tracking when acting as target aircraft. At the end of 1980 the FRADU still had 26 Hunter GA/PR11s and T8s on its inventory.

Top and above: FR10 XG168 of No 79 Squadron with *(above)* nose detail showing camera installation. Note 'eyelid' on nose tip camera. *APN*

Top right: After service with the RAF College of Air Warfare as a Mk 4, WV380 was converted to a GA11 for the Royal Navy. *BAe-Kingston*

Centre right: GA11s of the Fleet Air Arm at Farnborough; note nose wheels retracting. *Peter Gilchrist*

Bottom right: XE689, a GA11 converted from a No 67 Squadron Mk 4. *Peter Gilchrist*

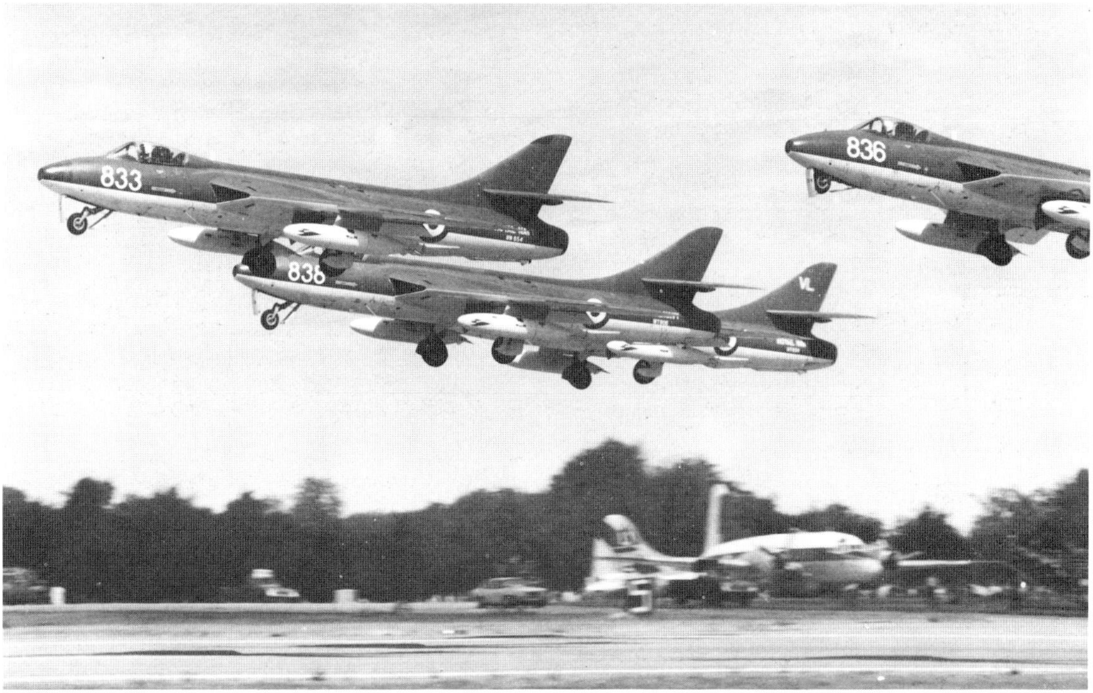

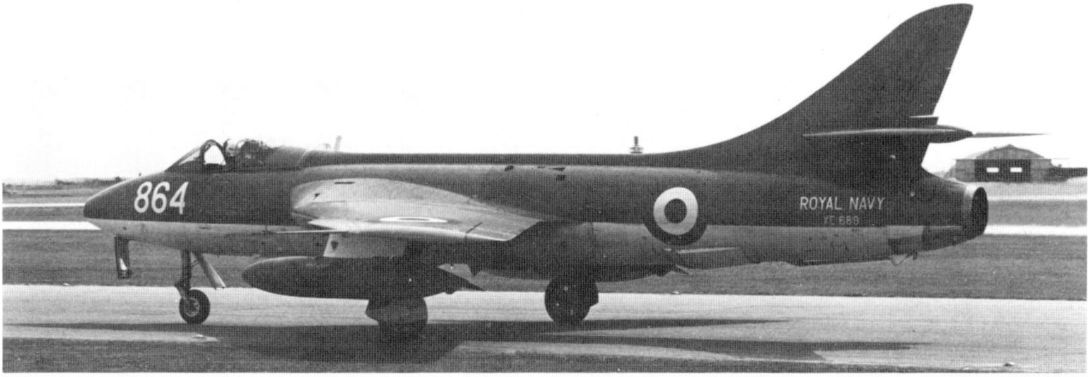

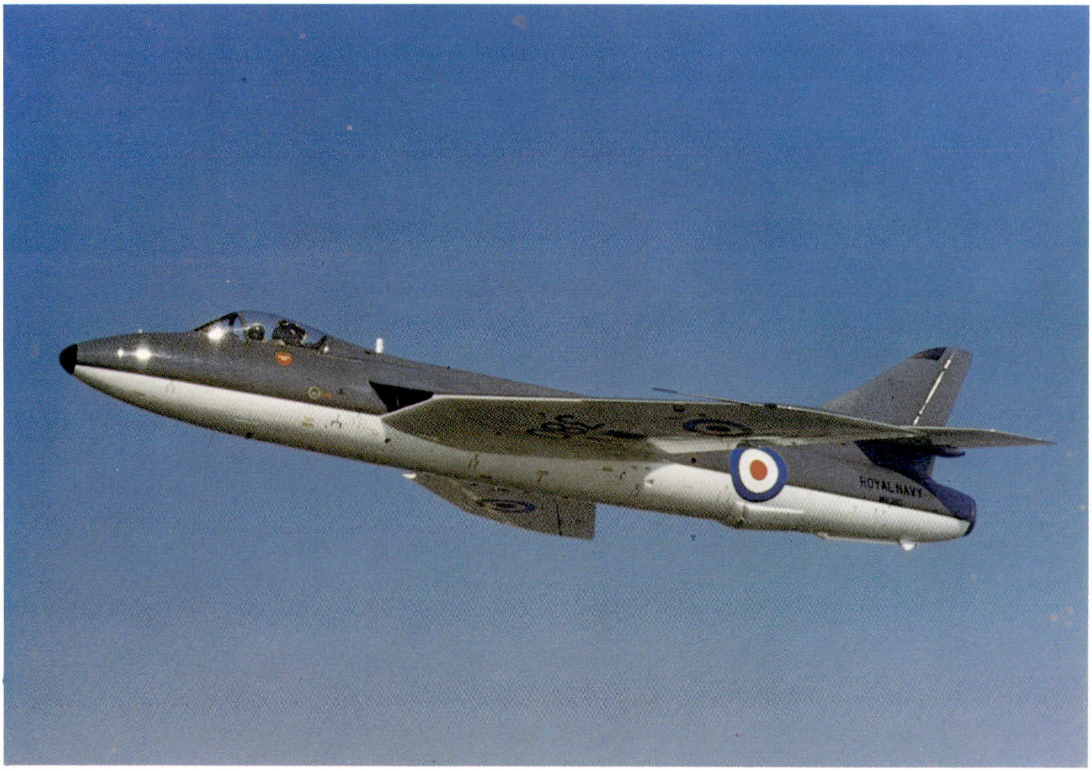
ROYAL NAVY

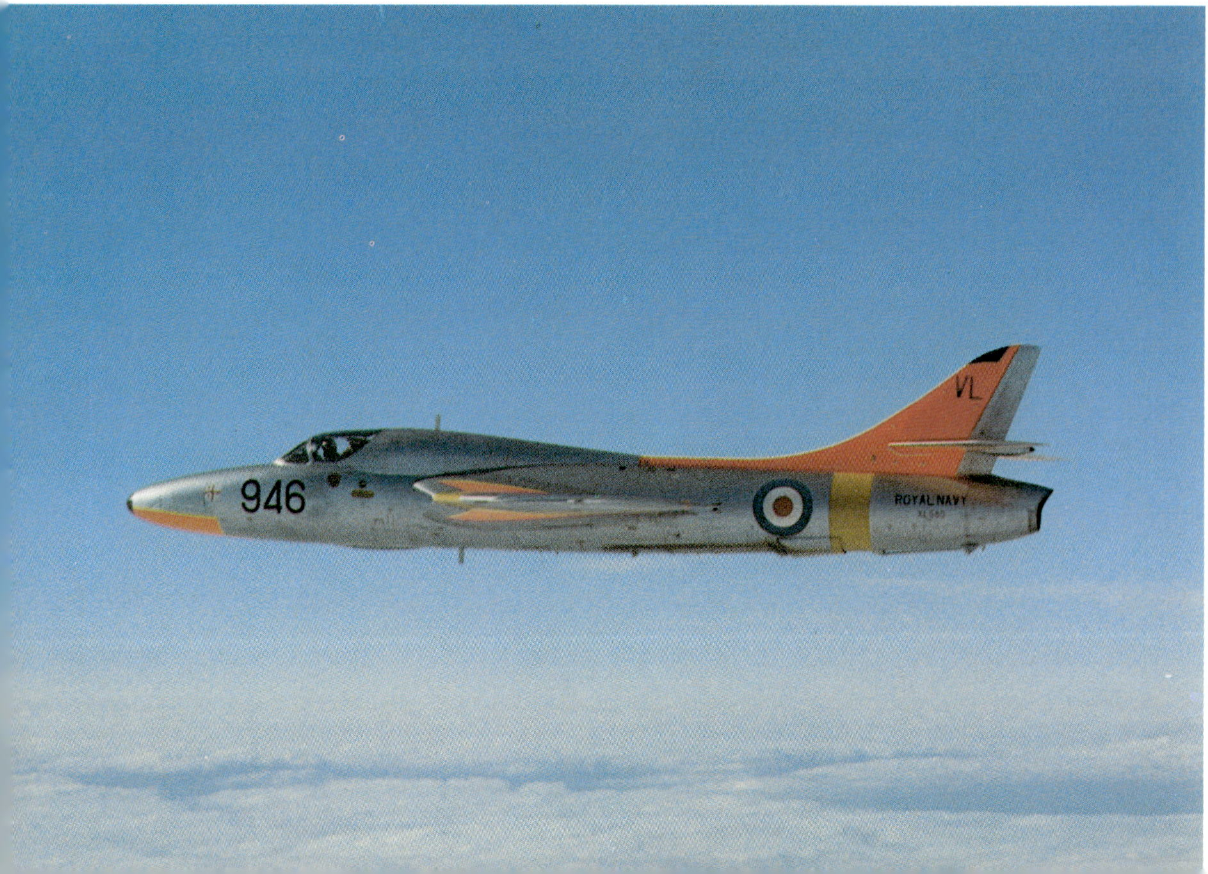
VL
946
ROYAL NAVY

Top left: Hunter GA11 WV380 of the Fleet Air Arm. This aircraft was delivered to the Swiss Air Force in November 1972 as a Mk 58A. *BAe Kingston*

Bottom left: Hunter Mk 8 of No 764 Squadron, Fleet Air Arm. *BAe Kingston*

Above: Iraqi Hunter Mk 59 — this designation was given to Hunter F6s converted to FGA9 standard and sold to Iraq between March 1964 and May 1965. *BAe Kingston*

Below: Singapore Air Force Hunters' '536' and '538'. The former started life as F4 XF950 and was delivered to Singapore as a T57A in April 1973; the latter, F4 XF369 went as an FR74B in the same month. *BAe Kingston*

5
Hunters that Never Were

In 1950, several months before the prototype P1067 made its first flight, the thoughts of the Hawker project team were already turning to the development of a successor with a supersonic performance. The proposal was to employ a basic P1067 fuselage, lengthened to accommodate an afterburning Rolls-Royce Avon RA14 turbojet and married to a new wing with a thickness/chord ratio of only 7.5% and swept 52 degrees at the leading edge.

Serious design work on the project, which was allocated the designation P1083, began in November 1951, and an Instruction to Proceed was received by the Company on 26 February 1952 for the construction of a prototype, WN470, which was expected to be ready to fly before the end of 1953. A draft specification was drawn up around the P1083 project and issued on 18 April 1952; this was followed, on 12 June, by a meeting of Company, Air Staff and Ministry of Supply representatives to discuss a possible production schedule. By this time the airframe of the fourth prototype P1067 was already undergoing modification and construction of the new wing had begun, the starboard section being completed in the following October. Shortly afterwards, a mock-up of the afterburning RA14 engine was also married to a mock-up of the P1083 rear fuselage.

It was now estimated that the prototype P1083 would be ready for flight by July 1953, and work was proceeding on a number of design changes that were to be incorporated in production aircraft. It was eventually decided that the production model was to be powered by a Rolls-Royce Avon RA19 engine developing 12,500lb st with reheat; this meant some substantial redesign of the rear fuselage to accommodate the RA19s larger jet pipe. Several alternative powerplants were considered, including an afterburning Armstrong Siddeley Sapphire ASSa4 (Project No P1095), but the Rolls-Royce engine was considered to offer the best performance and to be the most suitable for adaptation to the P1083 design. Two more schemes for alternative powerplants were considered briefly and then rejected; these were the P1097, a P1083 with an RB106 engine, and the P1090, which envisaged the use of a de Havilland Gyron.

Considerable thought was also given to increasing the P1083's endurance, and it was decided to install integral wing type tanks similar to those then being developed for the Hunter F4. These, together with additional fuel tankage space in the rear fuselage, would have given the production P1083 a total internal fuel capacity of 600gal, compared with the prototype's capacity of 440gal. Armament for the proposed production aircraft was standardised on four 30mm Aden cannon of 150 rounds each, while a slab-type tailplane was adopted in preference to an all-flying tail, which had produced some stability problems during wind tunnel testing. With a full load of fuel, the estimated all-up weight of the P1083 was 20,000lb. A flight profile that included a one-minute engine run-up at one-third power, take-off and acceleration to climb speed at sea level, climb to 50,000ft, 10 minutes combat at that altitude and cruise at the same altitude until 40gal of fuel remained for descent and landing, gave the aircraft an estimated endurance of 1.25 hours, taking into account the use of reheat for take-off, acceleration, climb and combat. At a loaded weight of 17,700lb with half fuel, the P1083 had an estimated maximum speed of 820mph (Mach 1.08) at sea level, 790mph (Mach 1.2) at 36,000ft, and 690mph (Mach 1.05) at 55,000ft. Estimated initial rate of climb was 50,000ft/min at sea level, 28,700ft/min at 20,000ft, and 5,400ft/min at 50,000ft, while estimated service ceiling was 59,500ft. Time to 30,000ft at a normal loaded weight of 20,000lb was estimated to be 1min 57sec, and to 55,000ft 5min 12sec from start of the take-off roll. Dimensions of the aircraft included a wingspan of 34ft 4in, a length of 45ft 10.5in, a height of 13ft 2in, and a wing area of 358sq ft.

In June 1953 the prototype P1083 was 80% complete and there were hopes that WN470 would be ready in time to fly in the SBAC Show at Farnborough the following September. Then came the blow: on 22 June Hawkers received warning that the P1083 was now considered by the Air Staff to have less development potential than a rival design, the Supermarine Type 545, and that Air Staff attitudes had hardened against the choice of the afterburning Avon RA19 powerplant. The final death-knell was sounded on 13 July 1953, when the P1083 was officially cancelled.

Ironically, so was its competitor, two years later. Just as the P1083 had been based on the design of the Hunter, Supermarine's Type 545 had been based on the design of the Type 541 Swift, although the 545 bore far less resemblance to its predecessor than did the Hawker project. The 545's most distinctive feature was its crescent-type wing planform, the leading edge sweep ranging from 50 degrees at the root through 40 degrees at mid-point to 30 degrees at the outer portion. The aircraft, which was to have been powered by a Rolls-Royce Avon RA14 engine developing 9,500lb st

HAWKER P.1083

Type. Single-seat interceptor fighter. **Project Status.** Prototype partially complete by mid-1953 but contract cancelled.

Powerplant. One Rolls-Royce Avon R.A.19R. with 1,800°K reheat.

Weights. Normal loaded weight, 20,000 lb. (9 070 kg). Half-fuel weight, 17,700 lb. (8 027 kg).

Dimensions. Wing span, 34 ft. 4 in. (10.46 m); length, 45 ft. 10½ in. (13.98 m); height, 13 ft. 2 in. (4.01 m); wing area, 358 sq. ft. (28.26 m²); quarter-chord sweepback, 48.6°.

Performance. At half-fuel weight. Maximum speed at sea level, 820 m.p.h. (1 317 km/h = 1.08M); maximum speed at 36,000 ft. (11 000 m), 790 m.p.h. (1 273 km/h = 1.20M); sea level rate of climb, 50,000 ft./min. (254 m/sec.); service ceiling, 59,500 ft. (18 000 m); take-off distance to clear 50 ft. (15 m), 1,040 yds. (950 m).

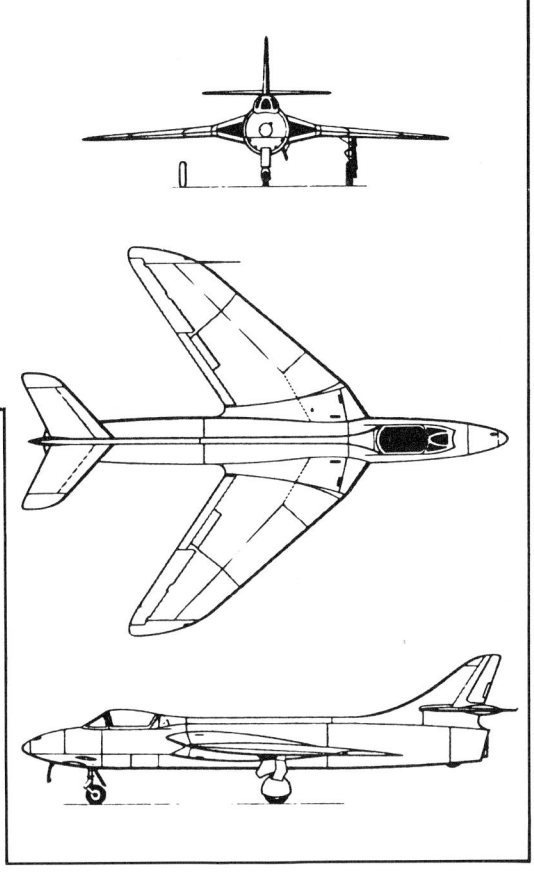

Above: Three-view of the Hawker P1083.

and 14,500lb st with full reheat, would have had an estimated maximum speed of 1.3M, with a service ceiling of 55,000ft and an endurance similar to that of the P1083. In the event, the prototype Supermarine 545, XA181, was almost complete when it was cancelled in 1955, and further development of a 2.0M derivative powered by a Rolls-Royce RB106 engine was also abandoned.

The cancellation of both the Hawker P1083 and the Supermarine 545 was a serious blow not only for the firms involved, but also for the Royal Air Force and the British aircraft industry's military aircraft potential. It was to be another six years after the cancellation of the P1083 that the RAF introduced a fighter with full reheat, the Gloster Javelin, and 1960 before the Service's first supersonic interceptor, the English Electric Lightning, entered squadron service.

More serious still, by 1960 a number of NATO air forces which by now had been operating the well-tried Hunter for some time were beginning to look for a supersonic successor, and since Britian had no suitable aircraft to offer they were compelled to turn to the United States to fill the gap. Had the operational version of the P1083 been available, there seems little doubt that it would have captured a sizeable slice of the market that was eventually cornered by the North American F-100 Super Sabre. Another, less obvious loss caused by the cancellation of the P1083 and its rival involved flight experience with supersonic wing sections; once again, several years were to pass before this deficiency could be made good.

The story of the P1083 did not quite end with its cancellation in 1953. The fuselage of the unfinished prototype, after suitable modifications, took to the air on 22 January, 1954 as the Hawker P1099 XF833 — the prototype Hunter F6.

Another Hunter-based project was the P1091, which envisaged the fitting of a delta wing to a Hunter F4 fuselage. The suggested powerplant was a Rolls-Royce Avon RA14R and design studies were carried out in 1951 in parallel with A. V. Roe and Company, but no further development was undertaken. The P1100, which also reached project design stage, envisaged a supersonic mixed-powerplant Hunter with an RA24 turbojet and two auxiliary rocket motors, while the P1102, which was schemed only, was a Hunter with a thin wing. In 1955 technical studies were also carried out for a time on two possible all-weather Hunter variants, the P1114 with a Rolls-Royce Avon and the P1115 with an Armstrong-Siddeley Sapphire, and the following year detailed design studies were well under way on the P1120, a Hunter advanced trainer. The last Hunter proposal, the P1128 of 1957, was a private venture six-seat high-speed transport powered by two rear-mounted Bristol Orpheus turbojets, but this reached the project design stage only.

Left: PN-NLH, a T7 sold to the Lucht-en-Ruimtevaartlaboratorium, Amsterdam, seen at the Hunter's 25th anniversary meet at the International Air Tattoo, Greenham Common, 31 July 1976. *Martin Horseman*

Below: Hunter T7 XL567 '84' of No 4 FTS. *BAe Kingston*

6
Hunters for Export

Abu Dhabi (United Arab Emirates)

In February 1969, the Abu Dhabi Air Force placed an order with Hawker Siddeley for the supply of seven single-seat Hunters to be brought up to full FGA9 standard, and these were delivered in 1970 under the designation FGA76 to form a ground-attack squadron. At the same time, an order was also placed for three fighter-reconnaissance Hunters, designated FR76A, and for two Hunter trainers, brought up to Mk 66B standard and designated T Mk 77. All the Hunters supplied to Abu Dhabi were refurbished ex-RAF Mk 4s or Mk 6s with the exception of the two trainers, which were ex-Netherlands machines. Eight FGA76s/76As and the two trainers were still in service at the end of 1980, with the ground-attack squadron at Sharjah, and despite the arrival of more modern equipment in the form of 32 Mirage 5 strike/interceptors there are no plans at the time of writing to withdraw the Hunter ground attack aircraft from service.

Belgium and Holland

In 1953, the Hawker Hunter Mk 4 was selected under the United States Government's off-shore procurement scheme to replace the Meteor Mk 8 in service with day-fighter units of the Royal Netherlands and Belgian Air Forces, and the following year an agreement was signed whereby the fighter was to be licence-built by Fokker in Holland and Avions Fairey and SABCA in Belgium, initial contracts calling for the manufacture of 192 Belgian and 156 Dutch machines. The first Belgian Mk 4s were delivered to the 7th Wing at Chievres in 1956, and in 1957 the 1st Wing at Beauvechain and the 9th Wing at Bierset also gave up their Meteors in favour of the new aircraft.

In all, 112 Hunter 4s were built in Belgium, and in 1958 these were followed by 52 examples of the more powerful Mk 6. Ninety-two Mk 4s were subsequently brought up to Mk 6 standard, so that by the end of 1959 144 Hunter Mk 6s were in service with the Belgian Air Force. These equipped the 7th and 9th Wings; the 1st Wing operated its Hunter 4s for about a year, after which it received Avro Canada CF-100s and became an all-weather fighter wing. The 9th Wing had completely re-equipped with Hunter 6s by the middle of 1959, but the following year it was disbanded to re-form as a surface-to-air missile wing with Nike SAMs. Most of the Hunters which had served with the 1st and 9th Wings were placed in storage, the 7th Wing now being the sole Belgian Air Force Hunter

Below: Belgian Hunter F6 of the 7th Fighter Wing. *RBelAF*

58

Left: RNethAF T7. This aircraft was part of a batch of 20 diverted to Holland from a cancelled British Air Ministry contract. *BAe-Kingston*

wing, with some 50 aircraft on strength, but this unit also disbanded in 1963. Ninety-four ex-Belgian Hunters were subsequently purchased by Hawker Aircraft Ltd for refurbishing and resale overseas. Perhaps the most famous of these was Mk 6 serial IF-19, which was badly damaged in a wheels-up landing after the pilots had ejected; repaired by Hawkers and married to another nose section, the airframe was registered G-APUX and this aircraft became the Company's famous and much-travelled two-seat T Mk 7 demonstrator, which was spun by Bill Bedford over Farnborough and later leased to Iraq. Most of the other repurchased aircraft were brought up to FGA9 standard, and subsequent overseas sales included four to Kuwait as F Mk 57s and 44 to Iraq as F Mk 59s. The Hunter's safety record in Belgian Air Force service was excellent, only about 12 machines being written off through accidents.

Production of Hunter Mks 4 and 6 by Fokker totalled 220 aircraft, which equipped Nos 324 and 325 Squadrons at Leeuwarden and No 327 Squadron at Soesterburg. Hunter Mk 4s were also allocated to No 322 Squadron, which in 1960 was rushed out to Dutch New Guinea to reinforce the relatively weak Netherlands forces in the area, faced with confrontation against Indonesia. They remained there until 1962, when Dutch New Guinea was transferred to Indonesia and the threat of open warfare receded. At home, the RNethAF Hunters were gradually replaced in front-line service by the F-104G Starfighter from 1963, although the Hunter F6 remained on the active inventory in small numbers until the late 1960s. Forty-seven Mk 6s were repurchased by Hawker Siddeley between 1962 and 1970 for refurbishing and resale overseas.

The Royal Netherlands Air Force also bought 20 Hunter T7 trainers, 10 of which were diverted to Holland from a cancelled Air Ministry contract (XM117-XM126). The first Dutch T7 flew on 19 March 1958 and all 20 machines had been delivered to the Hunter OCU at Twente by February 1959. Ten aircraft were later repurchased by Hawker Siddeley for resale overseas.

Chile

Following the sale of Hunters to Peru in 1955-56, Hawker Siddeley made determined efforts to interest other Latin American air forces in the type, and in October 1966 a contract was signed with Chile for the supply of an initial batch of 15 refurbished Mk 6s (ex-RAF, Netherlands and Belgian machines) under the designation FGA Mk 71, all brought up to full FGA9 standard. The same contract also called for the delivery of three fighter-reconnaissance Hunters under the designation FR Mk 71A; these were all ex-RAF Mk 6s brought up to FR10 standard. This first order was followed by another, in September 1969, for an additional nine FGA Mk 71s.

Four two-seat Hunter trainers of Mk 66A standard, designated T Mk 72, were also ordered under the 1966 contract. Three were ex-RAF and ex-Netherlands Mk 6s and the fourth was the venerable G-APUX demonstrator. All were delivered during 1967-68. A fifth T72 was added to the inventory later.

All Chile's Hunters served in the fighter-bomber and operational training role with the Fuerza Aerea de Chile's Grupos 8 and 9 at Antofagasta, and about 20 were still airworthy in 1980. Chile's Hunter fleet, however, suffered from the UK arms embargo imposed in 1974 and only lifted after six years, which resulted in a critical shortage of Hunter spares. Reports, at the time of writing, suggest that Chile is considering re-engining its surviving Hunters with either a French or an American powerplant, and approaches are known to have been made to overseas Hunter users, including India, in a bid to obtain more aircraft.

Denmark

On 3 July 1954, Hawker Aircraft Ltd received their second overseas Hunter order in rapid succession when a contract was signed with the Danish Government for the delivery of 30 Mk 4 standard aircraft to the Royal Danish Air Force. The following year, Mk 4 WW591 went to Denmark for evaluation, and its demonstration flights left the Danes in no doubt that the Hunter was the aircraft they needed for the day

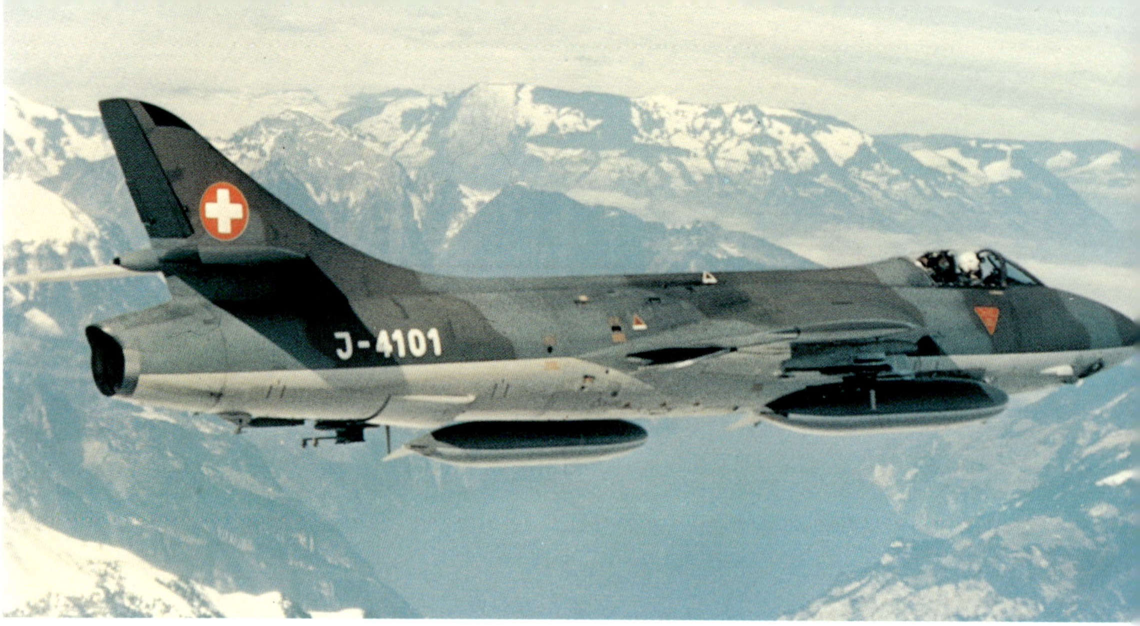
J-4101

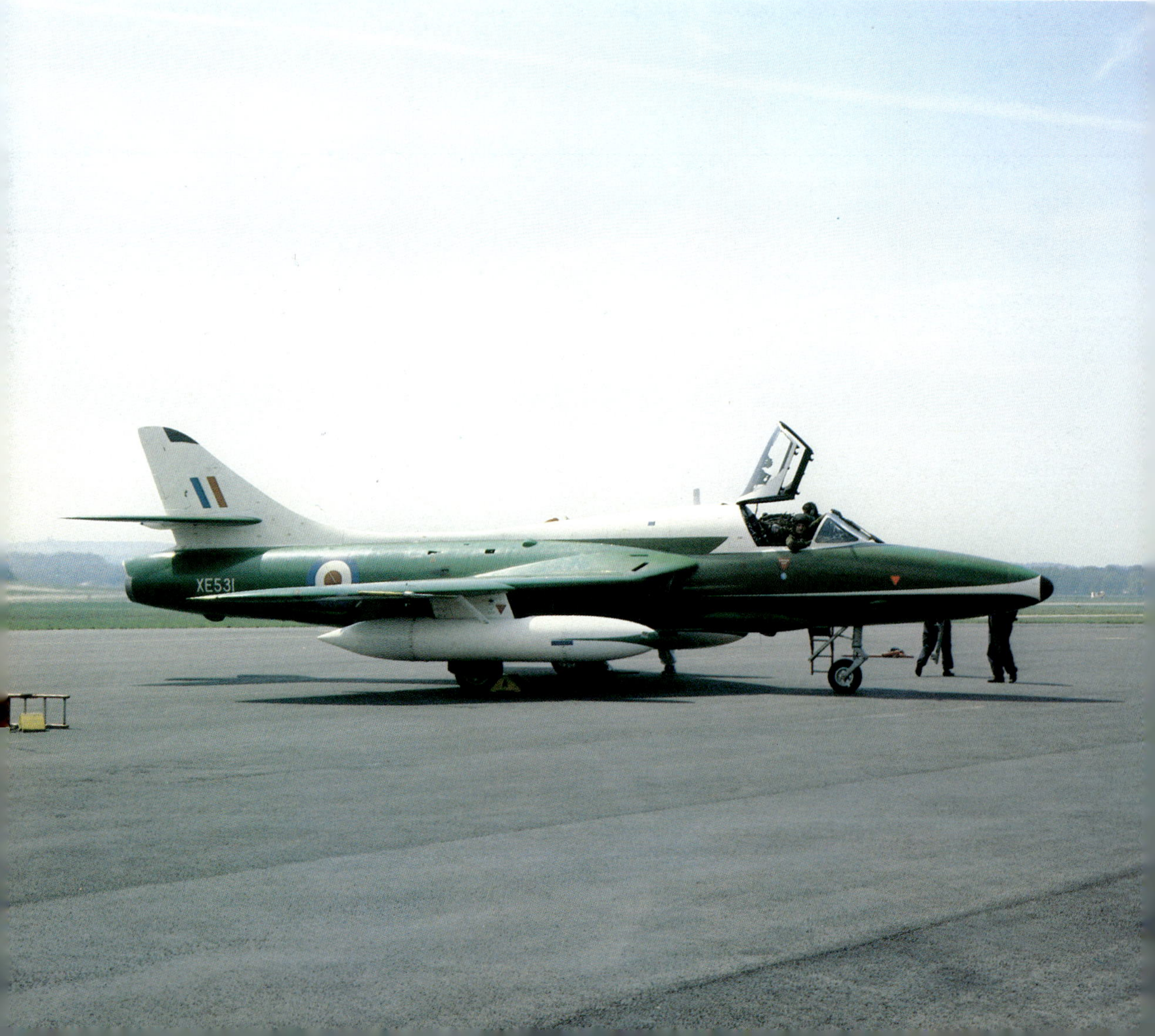
XE531

Top left: Swiss Mk 58A J-4101. This aircraft, ex-WT713, started life as a F Mk 4, became a GA11 and finally was converted to FGA9 standard for sale to Switzerland. *BAe Kingston*

Bottom left: Hunter T12 XE531, the fly-by-wire trials aircraft at RAE Farnborough which crashed in early 1982. *Peter Gilchrist*

Above: Hunter GA11 '865' of the Fleet Requirements and Aircraft Direction Unit (FRADU) at Yeovilton. *BAe Kingston*

Below: Detail of nose markings on a Hunter FGA9 of No 58 Squadron at Greenham Common, 31 July 1976. *Martin Horseman*

Above: Hunter T Mk 53 of the Royal Danish Air Force, one of two delivered in 1958. *RDAF*

Left: Danish F Mk 51s; the second aircraft from the camera, E417, crashed in June 1956. *RDAF*

defence of their Baltic coastline. WW591 became, in fact, the first Hunter formally to enter service with the RDAF, on 30 January 1956.

All 30 Hunters, designated Mk 51, were in service by mid-August 1956 with the RDAF's No 724 Squadron, at that time stationed at Aalborg. The aircraft were originally fitted with Rolls-Royce Avon Mk 115 engines, but these were later modified to eliminate engine surge problems during gun firing. The Hunters, all of which were built at Kingston, were flown from Dunsfold to Vaerlose in the first instance before joining their unit.

In June 1958 No 724 Squadron moved to Karup, but was there only a short time before it moved again, this time to Skrydstrup, in order to be closer to its operational area on the edge of the Baltic. To provide wider air defence coverage, one flight was based permanently at Vaerlose until 1966, when the Hunter force began to be run down. This was due mainly to restrictions imposed by the Danish Defence Act of 1966, which resulted in a reduction of squadron strengths and, as far as the Hunter was concerned, in a

lack of funds to purchase necessary spare parts. Some Hunters were placed in storage and slightly damaged aircraft were cannibalised to keep the remainder flying, but by November 1973 No 724 Squadron had an effective strength of only 10 aircraft. These, too, were placed in storage at Aalborg when the unit was disbanded on 31 March 1974; one aircraft was retained for display in the RDAF Museum, and the remainder (20 in number) were eventually bought back by Hawker Siddeley.

In addition to the Mk 51s, the RDAF also used four Hunter trainers. The first two of these, designated T Mk 53, were delivered late in 1958 and were similar to the RAF's T7s, being powered by Avon 122 engines. The major difference was that they lacked wing leading edge extensions, as did the Danish Mk 51s. Two T Mk 7s were purchased from the Royal Netherlands Air Force in December 1968 and March 1969 and modified to Danish standards.

India

September 1957 was a significant milestone in the Hunter's career, for during that month Hawker Aircraft Ltd received their first overseas order for the Mk 6 version of the fighter, an initial contract being signed with the Indian Government for the delivery of 160 examples under the designation F Mk 56. The first 32 of these were in fact already being built as Mk 6s for the RAF under a Ministry of Supply contract, but were completed as Mk 56s for the Indian order. The next 16 machines were ex-RAF Hunter Mk 6s overhauled at Maintenance Units, while the 49th and subsequent aircraft were all newly-built to Indian Air Force standards, modifications including gun blast deflectors, tail parachutes and — later in the production batch — underwing hard points for the carriage of 230gal drop tanks.

The first Mk 56 for India (BA201) flew on 11 October 1957. Several Indian Air Force pilots were already undergoing conversion training at Dunsfold and deliveries began as soon as this was completed, the Hunters, each fitted with four 100-gallon drop tanks, being ferried in stages by RAF pilots to Karachi and then allocated to Nos 7, 17, 20 and 27 Squadrons of the Indian Air Force at Ambala and Poona. Three follow-on orders for Mk 56s were subsequently placed, in 1965, 1967 and 1968, 53 aircraft — modified to Interim Mk 6/FGA9 standard — being delivered under the designation Mk 56A. The initial Hunter contract for India also covered the manufacture of 12 two-seat T Mk 66s, fitted with Rolls-Royce Avon 203 engines and twin 30mm cannon; the first of these, BS361, flew on 6 August 1958, and the first delivery took place in February 1959 following a protracted series of trials that led to the fitting of newly-designed gun blast deflectors. Ten more T Mk 66s were delivered under a second contract placed in 1960, and a further contract was placed in 1966 for the delivery

Top: Mk 56 for India (BA239) with underwing rocket pods.
BAe-Kingston

Above: Nose shot of Indian Mk 56 with 500lb bombs on underwing pylons. This aircraft is part of the initial batch, which were not fitted with gun blast deflectors. *BAe-Kingston*

of a further 12 machines. The latter, with a new avionics fit and equipped to carry 230gal drop tanks, were all modified ex-Netherlands Air Force Hunter Mk 6s and in Indian Air Force service were designated T Mk 66D. The Hunter trainers were allocated on the basis of two per squadron, the remainder being based at the Hunter Operational Conversion Unit at Ambala. Despite losses suffered during the Indo-Pakistan Wars of 1965 and 1971, about 100 Hunter F56/56As and T66s were still on the IAF inventory in 1980, serving with Nos 20, 27 and 37 Squadrons at Kalaikunda, but they were being gradually phased out with the arrival of first deliveries of Jaguar International.

Iraq

The Arab-Israeli war of 1956 precipitated considerable changes in the military atmosphere of the Middle East, with the Soviet Union making increasing inroads into what had up to that time been traditionally western arms markets. Between 1957 and 1960, Iraq, Syria, Jordan, Egypt and the Lebanon all embarked on major programmes to modernise their air forces in order to keep pace with a similar expansion in Israel, and it was no small tribute to the qualities of the Hawker Hunter that, in the face of stiff competition form other exporters, the British fighter was selected by three to those nations to from the backbone of their fighter/ground-attack squadrons.

The biggest Arab customer was Iraq, which received an initial batch of five ex-RAF Hunter Mk 6s, modified up to the latest standard, purchased with American funds, in April 1957; this was followed by ten more aircraft in December that year, and by the spring of 1958 Iraq's first Hunter squadron was fully operational at Habbaniyah, its pilots receiving conversion training in the United Kingdom with 229 OCU at Chivenor. The excellent service rendered by Iraq's first 15 Hunters led to further orders being placed in 1964-66 for an additional 42 aircraft; these came in two batches, one of 24 and the other of 18. The majority were ex-Belgian Mk 6s, with a few former Royal Netherlands Air Force machines, and all were refurbished by Hawker Siddeley and brought up to full FGA9 standard before delivery. Aircraft in the first batch were designated FGA Mk 59, and those in the second FGA Mk 59A.

In 1963 the demonstration Hunter trainer G-APUX was leased to Iraq for a year, following a tour of the Middle East, and Iraq subsequently received five two-seat T Mk 69 trainers, the first three in 1963-64 and the other two in 1965. All were ex-Belgian Mk 6s, converted and refurbished by Hawker Siddeley. Completing the total of Iraqi Hunters were four full standard FR10s, all converted Mk 6s returned to Hawkers from Belgium and designated Mk 59B in Iraqi service.

Iraq's Hunters saw comparatively little action during the Six-Day War of June 1967. Although the Iraqi Air Force was in a position to attack targets in Israeli territory, possessing aircraft with sufficient range, only one Iraqi bomber — a Tupolev Tu-16 — entered Israeli air space on 5 June and was shot down near Netanya. As a result of this attack, however, Israeli Mystéres and Mirages hit Habbaniyah with a surprise attack some hours later, destroying nine MiG-21s, five Hunters and an Il-14 transport on the ground. After that, the Iraqi Air Force took no further

Left: Three FGA9s of No 45 Squadron from RAF Wittering. *BAe Kingston*

Above: Iraqi Air Force Hunter FGA Mk 59 delivered in the mid-1960s. *BAe-Kingston*

part in the hostilities and the Israelis left it alone; Iraqi Hunters and other aircraft restricted their operations to flying CAP over the border.

In the autumn of 1980 the Iraqi Air Force still had some 30 Hunters on its active inventory in three squadrons, and there were reports that some of these had been in action in support of ground forces during Iraq's invasion of neighbouring Iran. The primary ground-attack role within the Iraqi Air Force's Support Command, however, has been progressively taken over by Soviet-supplied Su-7Bs and Su-20s.

Jordan

Undoubtedly the most professional of the Arab air forces to receive the Hunter was that of Jordan. The history of the Hunter in the Royal Jordanian Air Force dates back to 1958, when His Majesty King Hussein — himself a keen pilot — applied himself vigorously to the task of modernising his country's air arm. To form a solid nucleus 12 Hunters, all ex-RAF Mk 6s, were acquired and these formed No 1 Fighter Squadron at Mafraq. In 1964 the Hunter force was further increased with the delivery of eight refurbished ex-RAF FGA9s, which formed No 2 Squadron, while No 6 Squadron, fulfilling the role of an operational conversion unit, used three two-seat T Mk 66B trainers similar in standard to the Indian Mk 66. The first T Mk 66B delivery took place in 1960. For some months in 1965 the RJAF also used the company-sponsored demonstration aircraft, Hunter T Mk 66A G-APUX, but this was returned to the United Kingdom and subsequently delivered to Chile in 1967.

The RJAF's Hunters went into action for the first time on 21 December 1964, when Israeli Mirages penetrated several miles into Jordanian territory. They

65

were engaged by four Hunters of No 1 Squadron, whose pilots claimed two confirmed kills over the much faster French-built jets for no loss to themselves. The next day the Israelis claimed that the Jordanian aircraft had penetrated Israeli air space and had been chased off by the IAF, a story that was completely refuted by a Royal Air Force officer who was on attachment to the RJAF and who followed the whole incident on radar.

On 11 November 1966, Israeli air and ground forces launched a strong attack against the village of Samu inside Jordan, which had been used as a jumping-off point by Palestinian guerrillas on their raids into Israel. Four RJAF Hunters made a gallant interception of a much larger number of IAF Mirages and in the ensuring air battle, which came down almost to ground level, one of the Hunters was shot down. The pilot, Lieutenant Salti, used his ejection seat but he baled out at too low an altitude and was killed the first Jordanian pilot to lose his life in combat. The other Hunters claimed possible kills on two Mirages during this engagement, but these were unconfirmed.

The Six-Day War of June 1967 started badly for the RJAF, because its sole early warning radar station at Ajlun was destroyed early in the day by the Israeli Air Force. This left the RJAF without any proper air defence system. Nevertheless, the RJAF Hunters pressed home several determined attacks on targets in Israeli territory, being the first aircraft of any of the Arab air forces to do so; at 10.30, for example, four Hunters of No 2 Squadron at Mafraq strafed the Israeli forward airstrip at Kefar Sirkin, just over the border, knocking out two Piper Super Cubs and a number of vehicles. The Hunters returned to their base to find it under attack by IAF Mirages, which the Jordanian pilots promptly engaged. One of the Hunters was quickly shot down; the pilot ejected and broke his back. All the others were hit, but managed to make their escape.

The IAF strike on Mafraq resulted in the destruction of several Hunters on the ground, including two which had been lined up on the runway awaiting permission to take off. The pilot of one of these was killed as he was trying to get out of his aircraft; he was the only Jordanian pilot to die in the Six-Day War.

During subsequent air attacks the IAF destroyed all but four of Jordan's Hunter force. The Hunter pilots made a few interceptions and, according to official RJAF records, claimed a total of four Israeli aircraft confirmed destroyed and two probably destroyed. With the RJAF Hunter squadrons all but wiped out, HM King Hussein ordered their pilots to neighbouring Iraq, where they were attached to Iraqi Air Force Hunter squadrons for the duration of hostilities.

The RJAF's Hunters might well have achieved more during the war of 1967 had it not been for the fact that the most experienced pilots were on leave, having been on an F-104 Starfighter conversion course in the United States and only returned to Jordan on the day before the Israelis attacked. Once the ceasefire was implemented the Jordanians went to great efforts to replace their losses; 12 more Hunter FGA9s were acquired, including some ex-Iraqi machines, and these were complemented by a small number of F-104s. The Hunter was eventually phased out of RJAF service in 1974, being replaced in Nos 1 and 2 Squadrons by the Northrop F-5 and in No 6 Squadron (the Hunter OCU) by the Cessna T-37. In 1975, the Jordanian Hunters were transferred to the Sultan of Oman's Air Force.

The Hunter's record in Jordan was summed up by a senior RJAF officer, Colonel G. Smadi, who wrote to the author: 'In its 16 years of service with the RJAF the Hunter aircraft proved to be one of the finest aircraft ever flown by fighter pilots. It has faced great challenges and many setbacks, yet it has always proved to be most efficient'. It is interesting to note, too, that the RJAF formed a first-rate aerobatic team known as the 'Hashemite Diamond' with nine Hunters, and worked up a display sequence that became quite famous in the Middle East between 1964 and 1967.

Kenya

At the end of 1973, following a growth of strike potential in the air forces of neighbouring Ethiopia, Somalia and Uganda, the Kenya Government requested British aid in building up a small air strike force for territorial defence. As a result, six refurbished ex-RAF Hunter FGA9s and one Hunter T80 trainer were delivered in 1974. These aircraft operated out of Nanyuki air base and by 1979 attrition had reduced the FGA9 force to four aircraft. All Kenya's Hunters were withdrawn from service with the delivery of 10 Northrop F-5s late in 1979 and placed in storage pending disposal.

Kuwait

Although the Kuwait Air Force existed for several years prior to 1961 as an extension of the Security Department of the Government of Kuwait, it first came into official existence in the autumn of that year as a result of the need to protect the country's oilfields following the threat from Iraq. In 1963, the Kuwait Government signed a contract with Hawker Siddeley for the delivery of four ex-Belgian Mk 6s, refurbished to full FGA9 standard, and these were delivered in 1965 under the designation FGA Mk 57. Two Hunter trainers, also ex-Belgian machines converted from Mk 6s, were ordered at the same time, and an order for three more (two ex-Royal Netherlands Air Force and one ex-RAF) was placed in 1967. All Kuwait's

Hunters were placed in storage in the mid-1970s, following the delivery of Skyhawks and Mirages.

Lebanon

The third Arab country to standardise on the Hunter was the Lebanon, which received its first six aircraft — all refurbished ex-RAF Mk 6s — in October 1958.

Above: Hunter T67s awaiting delivery to the Kuwait Air Force. *BAe-Kingston*

These were followed by four more aircraft — all ex-Belgian — in 1965, brought up to full FGA9 standard by Hawker Siddeley Aviation and designated

Below: Destined for sunnier skies: Hunter FGA70s for the Lebanon on a murky morning at Dunsfold. *BAe-Kingston*

FGA70. The total of Hunters eventually delivered to the Lebanon reached 17, including a final batch of six ex-RAF Mk 9s delivered in 1975-76 to make up for losses. Some Lebanese Air Force Hunters are known to have been lost in action against the Israeli Air Force during the latter's periodic forays into Lebanese territory, but no accurate details exist of their combat record. In 1966 the Lebanese Air Force also used Hunter Mk 66A G-APUX for a time, but this aircraft was returned to the United Kingdom on the delivery of three T Mk 66Cs, all of them ex-Belgian Mk 6 conversions. Two of the latter, and the surviving FGA70s, were still in service at the end of 1980.

Oman

One of the last air arms to receive Hunters was the Sultan of Oman's Air Force, which in 1980 had 31 aircraft on its inventory, of which 15 were in storage. SOAF's Hunters were acquired from various sources; some were ex-RAF FGA9s, while others were the Jordanian machines transferred to Oman in 1975. Still others were obtained from Kuwait, including two T Mk 67 trainers, and SOAF also uses a small number of FR10s. Some of SOAF's Hunters are hybrids, with components of former RAF Mk 9s married to parts of ex-RJAF Mk 73s. The active Hunter force equips No 6 Squadron at Thrumrayt and the aircraft are flown by seconded Royal Air Force personnel. Although a squadron of Jaguars was formed in 1977, with a second squadron scheduled to form in 1983, it is likely that some of SOAF's Hunters will remain in service in the ground-attack role for some time to come.

Peru

The Peruvian order for 16 Hunter Mk 4 aircraft in 1955 was won by Hawker Aircraft Ltd in the face of fierce American competition, for South American air forces were then being offered surplus F-80 Shooting Stars and F-86 Sabres at very low prices. Peru's decision, after assessing the relative qualities of both the F-86F and the Hunter Mk 4, was to equip one squadron of the air force's Grupo 12 with each type, the Grupo's third squadron operating F-80C Shooting Stars.

The Mk 4s ordered by Peru were all ex-RAF machines, returned to Dunsfold in the closing months of 1955 for conversion to the latest standard, and the first modified machine, designated Mk 52, flew on 1 December that year. Deliveries to Peru were completed during 1956, the Peruvian pilots undergoing conversion training at Dunsfold. The Hunters equipped Escaudron Caza 14 at Talara and Limatambo, and bore the serial numbers 630-645. A few were still in service in 1980 as operational trainers, but in first-line service the Hunter Mk 52 was replaced

by the Mirage 5P, the first examples of which reached the Fuerza Aerea del Peru in 1968. After that date the Hunters were used in the ground-attack role until this was taken over from 1976 by the Sukhoi Su-22 'Fitter-C', which currently equips Grupo 12.

The Peruvian Air Force also used a single Hunter trainer, which was delivered in October 1959. This was a converted Mk 4, WT706, and differed externally from the standard T7 in having an aerial fairing on top of the fuselage a few feet behind the cockpit.

Qatar

In June 1969, following Abu Dhabi's lead, the independent Middle East state of Qatar placed an order with Hawker Siddeley for three single-seat Hunter ground-attack aircraft refurbished to Mk 9 standard. These aircraft were part of a batch of ex-Netherlands Mk 6s returned to the United Kingdom and were delivered under the designation FGA Mk 78. The same contract also called for the delivery of one two-seat trainer to Mk 66B standard; an ex-Netherlands T7 was refurbished and modified and entered Qatar service as a T Mk 79. This aircraft, and two of the FGA Mk 78s, were still in service at the end of 1980, based at Dohar on the Arabian Gulf. Flown and maintained by personnel seconded from the Royal Air Force, they are used to patrol the State's coastline and, at the time of writing, are to be augmented by six Alpha Jets.

Rhodesia (Zimbabwe)

In 1962, the Rhodesian Government placed an order for 12 ex-RAF Hunter Mk 6s to be refurbished and brought up to full FGA9 standard. The first of these was delivered in January 1963 and deliveries were completed the following year, before Rhodesia's unilateral declaration of independence. These aircraft equipped No 1 Squadron at Thornhill and bore the serial numbers RRAF 116-127. The Hunters saw extensive operational service in support of ground forces during anti-guerrilla operations in the 1970s, and nine were still in first-line service with the Air Force of Zimbabwe in 1980.

Saudi Arabia

In January 1966, the decision was taken to form a new Saudi Arabian air defence system based on British fighters and American surface-to-air missiles, and an order was placed with the British Aircraft Corporation for the supply of 34 Lightning F Mk 53s and two T Mk 55 trainers. At the same time, four refurbished Hunter Mk 6s and two Hunter T7s were also ordered and delivered in 1966 from existing stocks, these aircraft being used to train RSAF pilots as a lead-in to the Lightning conversion programme. The Hunters were withdrawn from service in the mid-1970s.

Above: T Mk 62 trainer in Peruvian Air Force colours. The blister behind the cockpit houses a UHF aerial.   *BAe-Kingston*

Below: Hunter FGA78s awaiting delivery to the Qatar Air Arm. *BAe-Kingston*

Singapore

In 1968, the Republic of Singapore ordered 12 Hunter FGA Mk 74 fighter-bombers and four FR Mk 74A reconnaissance fighters, all refurbished ex-RAF FGA9s, and these were delivered in 1970 to form the strike nucleus of the island's Air Defence Command (subsequently renamed the Republic of Singapore Air Force) in 1971. Later deliveries during the 1970s brought the RSAF's total of Hunter FGA74s to 31 aircraft. Seven two-seat trainers were also supplied under the designation T Mk 75; the first four were ex-RAF Mk 4s and T7s converted to take the more powerful Rolls-Royce Avon RA28 engine. The RSAF's Hunters equipped two attack squadrons, Nos 140 'Osprey' and 141 'Merlin', both of which were based at Tengah in 1980, and the FGA74s were equipped to carry Sidewinder AAMs on underwing pylons.

Sweden

Early in 1954, some time before the completion of the first Hunter Mk 4, the Swedish Government began negotiations for the delivery of 120 examples of the new mark, all to be powered by the Rolls-Royce Avon RA21 engine. The contract was signed on 29 June 1954 and the first machine of the Swedish order flew on 24 June the following year. Production of the Swedish Hunters was split between Kingston and Blackpool, the 24 aircraft built at Kingston bearing the serial numbers 34001 to 34024 and the remainder the serials 34025 to 34120. All the Hunters delivered to Sweden were originally fitted with Rolls-Royce Avon Mk 113 or 115 engines, but these were subsequently uprated to Avon Mk 119 and 121A standard.

The 120 Hunters, designated Mk 50s by Hawker Aircraft Ltd and J-34 in Flygvapnet service, were assigned to four day fighter squadrons and provided an important complement to the Flygvapnet's standard day fighter, the Saab J-29. The Hunters were eventually replaced by the Saab J-35 Draken, but numbers remained in service into the late 1960s in the operational training role. In 1958 several examples were used as test-beds for a reheat system developed by Saab Flygmotor, but this was found to produce no significant increase in the Hunter's performance and it was not adopted as a general modification.

Switzerland

After the last de Havilland Venom fighter-bomber was delivered to the Swiss Air Force in 1957, Switzerland sought to meet a pressing requirement for a replacement for the obsolete Vampire/Venom fleet by evaluating several modern combat types, including the American F-86 Sabre and the French Mystere IVA. In June and July 1957 Hawker Aircraft Ltd, keen to follow up their successes in other overseas fields by a big Swiss order for the Hunter, sent two demonstration aircraft — XE587 and XE588 — to Switzerland for competitive trials in performance, handling and weapons delivery, during which the British fighter emerged the clear victor. In fact, Swiss defence officials later expressed their astonishment at the Hunter's ability to perform a full range of flying manoeuvres within the relatively narrow confines of the valley at the foot of which Meiringen airfield was situated, and as a result the demonstration aircraft were awarded the Swiss Alpine Badge!

The initial Swiss order, signed in January 1958 was for 100 aircraft, based on the Hunter Mk 6 but incorporating a number of modifications. One of these was the fitting of a brake parachute, the need for which had been revealed during competitive evaluation in Switzerland; a parachute was first fitted to demonstration aircraft XE587 and later became standard on Hunter Mk 56s and Mk 58s, as well as on the RAF's FGA9. Another modification to the Swiss Hunters was the enlargement of the ammunition link containers to hold spent shell cases, a move that arose from the need to protect Swiss farmers from cascading metal in the vicinity of the confined mountain gunnery ranges.

The first 12 Hunters for Switzerland were ex-RAF Mk 6s, the first machine (J-4001) flying on 29 March 1958, but the remainder were all newly built. Two more batches each of 30 aircraft were ordered in 1971 and 1974; these were all refurbished machines and were delivered in their component parts to the Federal Aircraft Factory at Emmen, where final assembly took place. The first batch of 100 Swiss Hunters bore the designation F Mk 58, while the aircraft in the two subsequent batches — finished to FGA9 standard — were designated F Mk 58A. Among other modifications, these aircraft were equipped to carry the Sidewinder AAM on underwing pylons. Many of the earlier Mk 58s were also brought up to Mk 58A standard. In addition to the single-seaters, a small number of refurbished Hunter trainers were also delivered to Switzerland under the designation T Mk 68.

Over 100 Hunters were still on the Swiss Air Force's active inventory at the end of 1980, equipping the 1 Staffel at Dubendorf in the interception role as well as the 5 Staffel at Meiringen and the 4,7 and 21 Staffel at Mollis in the fighter-bomber role. It is likely that the Hunters will eventually be replaced by further orders for the Northrop F-5.

Top right: Designated Hunter Mk 50 by HAL and J-34 in Swedish service, this is one of 120 Mk 4 variants supplied to the Flygvapnet in the 1950s. *BAe-Kingston*

Bottom right: Early Swiss-built Hunter F Mk 58. *Swiss Air Force*

Right: A Swiss Hunter Mk 58A demonstrates its ability to operate from an autobahn. *Swiss Air Force*

Below: The Patrouille Suisse, the Swiss Air Force aerobatic team, in perfect formation over the Alps. *Swiss Air Force*

7
The Hunter Refurbishing Programme

It was no small tribute to the Hunter's robustness and flexibility that, of 2,500 aircraft delivered to customers throughout the world, over one-fifth were converted or refurbished machines. Most of the early rebuilt Hunters were aircraft bought back from the Dutch and Belgian Air Forces by Hawker Siddeley, but the Royal Air Force's re-equipment programme of the early 1960s brought many surplus ex-RAF machines into the refurbishing scheme.

Early F4 conversions were relatively complex in that they involved major rebuilding to accommodate the large diameter Avon 200-series engine, the standard powerplant of the F6. Forward of the main spar the fuselage was compatible between marks, but aft of that the fuselage had to be completely rebuilt using standard F6 frames back to a modified frame 40a which formed the transport joint and engine attachment point. The wings produced fewer problems, being basically similar, while the cockpit canopy, fin and flying controls were common to both the F6 and F4.

A refurbished Hunter emerged from Kingston with virtually zero fatigue life, which meant that Hawker Siddeley were able to offer a potential customer a combat aircraft with a life of 3,000 hours at a fraction of the cost of a new and more modern type. Another factor that rendered the Hunter highly adaptable to the process was the high standard of interchangeability that was built into the design from the outset; the fact that the aircraft could be broken down into five major components was an important selling point, particularly in those countries which undertook licence manufacture of the type and those, like Switzerland, where aircraft were assembled from delivered component parts.

Hunters bought back from overseas sources for refurbishing were mostly flown into Dunsfold, where they were immediately made safe and defuelled, and a preliminary survey carried out. The aircraft was then split into its major components, with the tail unit forming a sixth section. Rear fuselages, together with wings, ailerons and flaps, were then sent to the Hawker factory at Bittesswell, where major jigs were held, while the tail surfaces and cockpit canopies went to Hamble.

(Many of the canopies had, in fact, been manufactured by the former Folland Aircraft Company plant there.)

The Avon engines were returned to Rolls-Royce for reconditioning, and although most engines were later remarried to the same airframe (in the case of F6 conversions) Rolls-Royce held a stock of engines in anticipation of market demands. Meanwhile, the preliminary survey carried out by Hawker's inspection department would have recorded the state of the aircraft and the work necessary to bring it up to a 're-delivery condition'. Each section of the airframe would then be classified under one of three headings: 'Discard and replace', 'Repair' or 'Modify'. Irrespective of the Hunter's previous owner, the manufacturer would then apply a serial number under the Class B registration system to identify the major fuselage sections for production and movement control purposes. As far as possible, Hawker Siddeley always tried to ensure that all components, once refurbished, came together again in a single aircraft; the obvious exception was when an old F4 or F6 had to be fitted with a two-seat nose section. In cases such as this, the removed single-seat nose section was sometimes stored against possible future use (to replace the nose of a damaged aircraft, for example), but usually it was declared redundant and scrapped.

While the major structural parts were being refurbished, the Hawker Siddeley designers would be working on the detailed requirements for turning — for example — a former Dutch Mk 6 into a Swiss Mk 58A, with all the necessary equipment modifications. These could often influence the unit cost of a refurbished Hunter substantially, so that in the mid-1970s an aircraft reworked up to full FGA9 standard would be resold for perhaps £500,000.

On arrival at the factory the repurchased Hunter would be stripped of all pipes and cables, while the various systems — oxygen, hydraulics, pneumatics etc — would be returned to the original manufacturer for reconditioning and re-certification. The airframes were stripped down to the primer coat and painted again after reassembly, while fuselage and wing skins were removed and replaced as necessary. One area that was reskinned as a matter of routine on later conversions was the underwing surface around the undercarriage pivot point.

Although British Aerospace has entered the 1980s with no announced plans to refurbish any more Hunters, some work of this kind is likely to be carried out in countries where the type is still serving, especially as one or two air forces (Zimbabwe among them) are reportedly seeking to acquire Hunters from other overseas users at the time of writing.

Right: Hunters, returned from RAF service to Hawker Siddeley, await refurbishing and eventual resale overseas. *BAe-Kingston*

8
India's Hunters in Combat

Indian Air Force Hunters saw limited action during the invasion of the Portuguese colony of Goa in 1961 and also against invading Chinese forces in the Himalayas late the following year, but the first real test came in 1965, during the short but bitter conflict between India and Pakistan that began in earnest on 6 September with an assault by the Indian Army towards Lahore, the capital of West Pakistan. By this time, attrition had reduced the number of serviceable IAF Hunters to 118, and right from the start these were heavily committed to both ground-attack and CAP operations, since large numbers of older Vampires and Ouragans had been hurriedly withdrawn from first-line IAF service following early combat losses.

Indian Air Force Hunters and Pakistan Air Force F-86 Sabres met in combat for the first time in the late afternoon of 6 September, when three F-86s attempted to attack the forward Indian airfield of Adampur, in the Punjab. South of Amritsar the Sabre pilots — all from No 11 Squadron — encountered four Hunters, flying slightly above them in close attack formation. Both sets of aircraft jettisoned their drop tanks and turned into each other; a fierce dogfight developed at tree-top height, the Hunters and Sabres reducing their speed to less than 200kts in a bid to out-turn one another. During this engagement the Sabre pilots claimed two Hunters destroyed and two damaged for no loss to themselves; these claims were unconfirmed, although all-India Radio subsequently announced that an IAF pilot had been decorated for bringing a badly damaged Hunter back to base at about the time of this action.

Shortly before dusk, another section of three Sabres, this time from No 5 Squadron, entered Indian territory to attack the airfield at Halwara. The Pakistani pilots were searching for their target in rapidly deteriorating visibility at 200ft when they sighted two Hunters, which they immediately engaged. According to the Pakistani account, one pilot, Flt Lt Cecil Choudhry, shot down one of the Hunters almost at once, then four more Hunters came up and the Pakistanis found themselves suddenly outnumbered. In the ensuing battle Choudhry claimed a second Hunter destroyed

and a third damaged, and stated that other Hunters had been destroyed by his fellow pilots Sqn Ldr Rafiqui and Flt Lt Hussain, both of whom were then shot down and killed. The Indian Air Force account of the action, however, is somewhat different:

'Patrolling over the Indian Air Base at Halwara on the evening of 6 September in Hunter F56s were Flt Lt D. N. Rathore and Flg Off V. K. Neb as No 2. At about 18.40 hours, when the sun had gone down and the horizon was lit only by twilight, Rathore, who was about three miles from the airfield, caught a flash in the air in the vicinity of the airfield.

'A second look confirmed that the base was under attack by Pakistani Sabres and that a dogfight was in progress with another section of two Hunters, led by Flg Off Ghandhi, who was also airborne on patrol duty, Rathore, warning Neb, immediately turned towards the airfield. In the first skirmish, however, one Sabre had been downed by ground fire, and the second had fallen to Ghandhi's guns.

'The remaining two Sabres were strafing the airfield and bombing it from a very low level. Jockeying for position was not difficult as the two Pakistani pilots were concentrating on their ground attacks. Getting behind the Sabre which was on his right, Rathore closed in to 1,000 yards, at the same time instructing Neb to take on the Sabre on his left. Overtaking his victim fast, Rathore closed in to 650 yards before opening fire. He saw the hits registering on the Pakistani Sabre, and it abandoned its ground attack. Closing in still further, Rathore fired again from 500 yards. This time the Sabre was mortally hit. It started banking to the left and then turned into the ground, exploding in a huge sheet of flame some five or six miles away from the airfield.

'Meanwhile, Neb had closed in behind the second Pakistani Sabre which, like the first one, was intent on strafing the airfield below. Neb, incidentally, had not done any air-to-air firing before and at the time of this engagement was still under operational training. Closing in on the Pakistani Sabre to about 400 yards he fired a burst. The Pakistani pilot at once abandoned his attack on the airfield and pulled up sharply. Neb, unsure of his accuracy because of lack of any practice, rapidly closed in to less than 100 yards and fired again on the sharply climbing Sabre, which presented a much better target this time. He saw pieces fly off the Sabre as his cannon shells found their mark on the Sabre's left wing. There was a puff of smoke which rapidly turned into a sheet of flame as the last of the four Pakistani Sabres disintegrated in mid-air and fell to the ground.'

The Indian Air Force admitted no Hunter losses during these battles of 6 September, although the

76

Pakistan Air Force subsequently released information on seven Hunters allegedly shot down on or around that date, and named two of the Indian pilots involved. The controversy will doubtless never be resolved.

Hunters were involved in fierce air combats on 7 September, when the Indian Air Force struck back hard with a series of attacks on the Pakistani airfield of Sarghoda. The first attack, by Dassault Mysteres, took the Pakistanis by surprise, but when the second wave — consisting of Hunters — approached Sarghoda the Sabres were airborne to meet them. The commander of the Sabre squadron involved in the subsequent engagements, Squadron Leader Alam, later gave this graphic account:

'As we were vectored back towards Sarghoda, Akhtar (Flg Off Masood Akhtar, Alam's No 2) called, "Contact — four Hunters", and I saw the IAF aircraft diving to attack our airfield, so I jettisoned my drops to dive through our own ack-ack after them. But in the meantime I saw two more Hunters about 1,000 feet to my rear, so I forgot the four in front and pulled up to go after the pair behind. The Hunters broke off their attempted attack on Sarghoda, and the rear pair turned into me. I was flying much faster than they were at this stage — I must have been doing about 500 knots — so I pulled up to avoid overshooting them and then reversed to close in as they flew back towards India.

'I took the last man and dived behind him, getting very low in the process. The Hunter can out-run the Sabre — it is only about 50 knots faster but has a much better acceleration, so it can pull away very rapidly. Since I was diving, I was going still faster, and as he was out of gun range, I fired the first of my two GAR-8 Sidewinder air-to-air missiles at him. In this case, we were too low and I saw the missile hit the ground short of its target.

'This area east of Sargodha, however, has lots of high-tension wires, some of them as high as 100-150 feet, and when I saw the two Hunters pull up to avoid one of these cables, I fired my second Sidewinder. The missile streaked ahead of me, but I didn't see it strike. The next thing I remember was that I was overshooting one of the Hunters, and when I looked behind the cockpit canopy was missing and there was no pilot in the aircraft. He had obviously pulled up and ejected and then I saw him coming down by parachute. This pilot was later taken prisoner.

'I had lost sight of the other five Hunters, but I pressed on thinking may be they would slow down. I had lots of fuel so I was prepared to fly 50-60 miles to catch up with them. We had just crossed the Chenab river when my wing man called out, "Contact — Hunters 1 o'clock", and I picked them up at the same time — four Hunters in absolutely immaculate battle formation. They were flying at about 100-200 feet at around 480 knots and when I was in gunfire range they saw me. They all broke in one direction, climbing and turning steeply to the left, which put them in loose line astern. This, of course, was their big mistake. If you are bounced, which means a close range approach by an enemy fighter to within less than about 3,000 feet, the drill is to call a break. This is a panic manoeuvre to the limits of the aircraft's performance, which splits the formation and both gets you out of the way of an attack and frees you to position yourself behind your opponent. But in the absence of one of the IAF sections initiating a break in the other direction to sandwich our attack, they all simply stayed in front of us.

'It all happened very fast. We were all turning very tightly — in excess of 5g or just about on the limits of the Sabre's very accurate A-4 radar ranging gunsight. And I think before we had completed more than about 270 degrees of the turn, at about 12 degrees per second, all four Hunters had been shot down. In each case, I got the pipper of my sight around the canopy of the Hunter for virtually a full deflection shot. Almost all our shooting throughout the war was at very high angles off — seldom less than about 30 degrees. Unlike some of the Korean combat films I had seen, nobody in our war was shot down flying straight and level.'

The Pakistani Sabre pilots had a healthy respect for the Hunter, but most seemed to agree that the British-built fighters were not flown to the limit of their performance and that Indian fighter tactics generally left a lot to be desired. Most, too, thought that in a straightforward dogfight the Sabre's armament of six 0.5in machine guns was better than the Hunter's 30mm cannon; the large bullet pattern from the machine guns often resulted in strikes being registered on the first burst, puncturing the Hunters' fuel tanks, and a second burst was then usually enough to set the fuel on fire.

The Hunter, however, had a far better thrust/weight ratio than the F-86F — 10,000lb of thrust at an all-up weight of 19,000lb compared with 6,000lb of thrust at 15,000lb for the Sabre, and during the climb and level flight the Hawker aircraft enjoyed a considerable performance advantage. It was also highly manoeuvrable at low speed, thanks to its split flaps, but it produced a higher induced drag than the Sabre and consequently tended to lose speed faster in a turn because the drag curve rose more sharply, and the extra thrust could not compensate for this. The Sabre pilots therefore preferred to fight on the turn, finding little difficulty in catching up with their targets and then tightening the turn at speeds as low as 120 knots to get inside their opponents' turning radius before opening fire. It was fortunate, for the Sabre pilots, that all

combats during the 1965 war between Hunters and F-86Fs took place at low level, for above 10,000 feet the Hawker fighter's performance was superior on all counts and the Pakistani tactics detailed above could not have applied.

The Pakistan and Indian Air Forces continued to trade punches throughout 7 September, the principal targets being forward airfields. As the day went on the Indian Air Defences appeared to become more co-ordinated and Hunters began to appear in strength to oppose the attackers; one attack by four Sabres on Kalaikunda airfield, for example, was intercepted by nine Hunters, which fell on the F-86s before they had a chance to jettison their drop tanks. One Sabre, flown by Flying Officer Khan of No 14 Squadron, was shot down almost immediately, but the others managed to get away.

From 8 September the Indian Hunters were heavily involved in close support operations and in attacks on Pakistani rolling stock and convoys close to the battlefront. Later, the Indian Defence Ministry issued an excellent account illustrating this type of operation, although it clearly describes one of the few real success stories of the ground-attack phase of the campaign: 'On 8 September four Indian Air Force Hunter pilots were briefed to carry out an offensive sweep over the Raiwind-Khem Karan sector. Composition of the formation was: Flt Lt C. K. K. Menon, leader; Flt Lt A. S. Kullar, No 2; Flt Lt D. S. Nagi, No 3 and subsection leader; and Sqn Ldr B. K. Bishnoi, No 4. The planes were armed with rockets and 30mm cannon.

'The section of four Hunters took off at 18.00 hours for the target area. The aircraft kept low, flying between 50 and 100ft above the ground, the fertile

green countryside of the Punjab passing under their wings as a blur.

'As the section approached Raiwind railway station, all four pilots saw a goods train which had pulled in. The leader decided that it was carrying military stores, because the locomotive was attached to that end of the train which pointed towards Kasur, in the battle area. Simultaneously the layout of the station and the area around the train was firmly implanted in his memory ... in about a second as the aircraft swept past.

'Menon as the leader asked his pilots whether they should take on the train. The reply was a unanimous affirmative. As the section had passed over the station anti-aircraft guns had opened up. To confuse the Pakistani gunners, and also to utilise the section of Hunters to the best effect against the Pakistani train,

Above: Part of the first batch of Hunter Mk 56s for India prior to delivery. *BAe-Kingston*

Menon decided to approach the goods train from a different direction. He therefore led the section well past the railway station till he was quite certain that the aircraft would be out of sight of those watching from the station. He then put his section in a wide left-hand turn to give the impression that the Hunters had missed seeing the goods train and to place his pilots in the best position for attack.

'The positioning of the section by Menon was excellent. As they pulled up and rolled to the left in the attacking dive, the section faced the train broadside, and was evenly spaced out along the entire length of the target. Going in first, through the mushrooming

79

flak, Menon concentrated on the extreme left of the train. He released his rockets at about 500ft and levelled out from the dive 100ft from the ground. He could not see his rockets hit the train, but Bishnoi, who as No 4 was the last to go in, could clearly see the effect of the other three pilots' strikes. Bishnoi saw Menon's rockets strike the wagons on the extreme left. The explosion lifted them off the rails and set fire to them.

'Kullar attacked the middle left of the target, and Bishnoi saw his rockets also hit their mark and turn that section of the train into a blazing inferno. As Kullar hurtled low over the train with ack-ack puffs chasing him, Nagi's rockets hit home in the middle right of the goods train. A powerful explosion ripped through the wagons. Putting the extreme right end of the train in his sights, Bishnoi then fired his own rockets from 400ft. He watched their smoke trails heading towards the target, but then he too was very low and had to level out of the dive. He went over the train at 100ft and then turned to see the effect of his attack. His rockets had also found their mark and the wagons at the extreme right were also burning furiously.

'By now explosions had started ripping the train apart, and the whole area was enveloped in smoke and flames. The section turned to fly up the railway line from Raiwind towards Kasur; Menon and Kullar still had some rockets left, and all four had their cannon ammunition intact.

'Nearing Kasur the pilots noticed a huge cloud of dust slightly to one side, so Memon led his section, flying very low, in that direction. Menon and Kullar picked up two groups of tanks as their target and pulled up to attack them. As their aircraft gained height rapidly, a murderous fire opened up on them from the ground. Undeterred, Menon went into a dive, latching on to one group of tanks, and fired his remaining rockets. Three tanks burst into flames. Kullar, who had followed Menon in the attack, concentrated on the second group of tanks and fired. He could not confirm the damage caused by his rockets but was certain that he had damaged a few. While Menon and Kullar were attacking the tanks, Nagi and Bishnoi took on some armoured vehicles with their cannon. Despite the very heavy ack-ack fire, they made two passes each at the armoured vehicles and saw a considerable number catch fire and blow up.

'All the while all four aircraft were being subjected to very heavy ground fire. Not only were the regular ack-ack guns firing, but also the anti-aircraft guns mounted on Pakistani tanks and other automatic weapons were blazing away at the Hunters. Nevertheless, Menon, after attacking the tanks, spotted two convoys of vehicles. Pulling up, he engaged the nearest with his cannon. Then, pulling up again, he attacked

the second convoy. In these two attacks, he saw that he had set fire to some 30 vehicles which, with their inflammable stores, were now bursting and exploding.

'Kullar, the No 2, after his rocket attack on the second group of tanks, pulled up again in the teeth of heavy ack-ack fire, ranged another tank in his gunsight, and went for it with his cannon. He managed to disable it.

'With their ammunition almost expended, the section turned back to base at very low level, re-forming at the same. Assessing the damage to their own aircraft, Menon found that his fuel state was lower than it should have been; ack-ack had punctured his port wing tank and the fuel had leaked out. Another bullet had damaged his airspeed indicator. Kullar had been slightly more unlucky; a bullet had found his main fuel tank and punctured it, so reaching his base was a touch-and-go affair. However, all four pilots reached base safely, although Menon had to be shepherded in because of his unserviceable ASI.'

According to the Indians, the goods train destroyed by the Hunters turned out to be unexpectedly important, because the Pakistani armour in the Khem Karan area was depending for replenishment on the supplies of petrol and ammunition it carried. The loss of the train meant that the Patton tanks in this sector were forced to go into action with only 30 shells each and a limited fuel supply, which caused their offensive to peter out and eventually led to their withdrawal with considerable losses.

Squadron Leader Bishnoi was in action again the following day, leading another section of four Hunters against gun positions and armour in the Khem Karan sector. The Hunters located a large concentration of tanks, armoured cars and soft-skinned vehicles and attacked the armour with their rockets through intense 40mm anti-aircraft fire, destroying several of the tanks. Their rockets expended, they then turned their attention to the other vehicles, which they attacked with cannon fire until their ammunition was used up.

As they were clearing the target area, the No 4 Hunter, flown by Flg Off Parulkar, was hit and the pilot wounded in his right arm, a bullet baring the flesh down to the bone. Despite severe loss of blood, Parulkar — shepherded by the others — regained base and made a safe landing.

Only once, during the 1965 war, did the Indian Air Force Hunters make contact with Pakistan's small force of Mach 2 F-104 Starfighters, and the result was interesting. It happened on 12 September, when two F-104s were scrambled from Sargodha to intercept a pair of Hunters at 25,000 feet over Lahore. The Starfighters quickly overhauled their targets at about Mach 0.85 and the Hunters broke hard left, one of them rolling over on its back and pulling through into a split-S manoeuvre while the other turned so tightly that it entered a high-speed stall. The lead F-104 pilot had by this time lost contact, but his No 2, Flt Lt Manzoor, pursued the second Hunter and tried to get into position either to release a Sidewinder AAM or to close the range sufficiently to enable him to use his Vulcan cannon. This proved impossible, for the Hunter continued to out-turn him and he was unable to bring his sights to bear. In the end, his fuel running low, Manzoor disengaged and cut in his afterburner, climbing to 36,000ft and returning to base.

One of only two high-level combats between Pakistani Sabres and Indian Hunters took place on 14 September, when both sides were fighting hard to establish air superiority over the battlefield. Two Pakistani pilots, Sqn Ldr Alam and Flg Off Shaukat, were patrolling at 20,000ft between the Indian Air-fields of Halwara and Adampur when they were inter-cepted by a pair of IAF Hunters, diving hard at about Mach 0.95. The Sabres broke towards them and turned behind the Hunters as they dived past, follow-ing them down until the Indian fighters separated in a vertical break at about 14,000ft. One of the Hunters carried on down; the other pulled up to 20,000ft with Alam still behind him. A turning fight developed, and Alam found that when he tried to match the Hunter at this height his aircraft flicked at about $6\frac{1}{2}$g. Reducing the turn a little, he managed to get the Hunter in his sights very briefly and hit it with two bursts of fire, reporting that the target then became 'a ball of fire'.

The second Hunter, meanwhile, had shot down Flg Off Shaukat, who ejected and was taken prisoner, and Alam now located and engaged this aircraft, diving behind it at Mach 0.95 and firing a Sidewinder. Alam's combat report stated that the missile hit the Hunter's wing root, which then began to smoke, but as he was now deep inside enemy territory and very short of fuel he dived down to tree-top level and returned to base without observing results.

The second high-level battle occurred in the after-noon of 20 September, and in fact marked the last fighter engagement of the three-week war. Four Sabres were engaged by an equal number of Hunters at 20,000ft between Kasur and Lahore; one of the Sabre pilots succeeded in damaging a Hunter, which he claimed had gone into the ground, but then the Sabres were engaged by four Gnats and in the ensuing battle one of the F-86s was shot down. Before the fight ended the Pakistanis claimed the destruction of a second Hunter, but neither of these claimed kills was admitted by the Indians.

Actual Hunter losses suffered by the Indian Air Force during the war of 1965 are difficult to assess, since in addition to those destroyed in air combat the Pakistanis claimed to have knocked out several during its airfield attacks. After the war, Pakistan went to considerable lengths to document its claims for Indian aircraft destroyed in action, and also admitted her own losses, both of which — concerning actions in which Hunters were involved — are listed below.

Indian Air Force Hunter Losses 6-22 September 1965

Date (Sept)	Pilot	Remarks
6	Flg Off Pingali	Shot down over Halwara by F-86. Pilot ejected safely.
6	Flg Off Ghandhi	Shot down over Halwara by F-86. Pilot ejected safely.
7	Sqn Ldr Bhagwat	Shot down by F-86 at Sargodha. Pilot killed.
7	Sqn Ldr Kackar	Shot down by F-86 at Sargodha. Pilow PoW.
7	Flg Off Brar	Shot down by F-86 at Sargodha. Pilot killed.
7	Sqn Ldr Rawlley	Shot down by F-86 at Sargodha. Pilot killed.
8	Flg Off Singh	Shot down by ground fire. Pilot PoW.
16	Flt Lt Bunsha	Shot down in Pakistan. Pilot killed.
20	Sqn Ldr Chatterjee	Shot down by F-86 over Taran Taran. Pilot killed.
22	Flt Lt Cariappa	Shot down by ground fire. Pilot PoW.
Date unknown	Flt Lt Ahnja	Hit by ground fire; died of wounds.
Date unknown	Flt Lt Chowdhry	Shot down by F-86. Pilot killed.
Date unknown	Flt Ltd Sharma	Shot down by F-86, ejected safely over India.

Pakistan F-86F Losses Attributed to IAF Hunters

6	Sqn Ldr Rafiqui	Shot down over Halwara. Pilot killed.
6	Flt Lt Hussain	Shot down over Halwara. Pilot killed.
7	Flg Off Afzal Khan	Shot down over Kalaikunda. Pilot killed.
16	Flg Off Shaukat	Shot down over Taran Taran. Pilot PoW.
19	Flt Lt Ahmed	Crashed after combat with Hunter; pilot injured.
20	Flt Lt Malik	Shot down in combat with Hunter over Lahore. Pilot ejected.

If the above figures are correct, then the Pakistanis established a slight ascendancy in Sabre-Hunter combat, shooting down nine Hunters for the loss of six Sabres. Total Indian losses from all causes clearly took the total of Hunters destroyed to a much higher level, the attrition being made good by a total of 53 more Mk56s ordered from Hawker Aircraft Ltd over the next four years.

The period of calm following the 1965 war was relatively short-lived, for in December 1971 India and Pakistan were once again drawn into conflict over the secession of East Pakistan (Bangladesh). At this time the IAF had 95 Hunters still in first-line service and these were widely employed on ground-attack operations from 3 December. On the 4th, 12 Hunter sorties were flown against the Pakistani airfield of Musroor, near Karachi, and the ground-attack aircraft claimed the destruction of eight Sabres and a B-57, although the actual damage inflicted was much less. One Hunter was shot down by an F-86 during this series of attacks, crashing into the sea. The Pakistanis claimed to have destroyed four more Hunters during operations that day, three of them shot down by F-86s and the fourth by an F-6 (Chinese-built MiG-19, 140 of which had been supplied to Pakistan) and there is no reason to doubt these claims, which were well documented.

On 5 December, the IAF intensified its attacks on Pakistani airfields at Lahore, Chanderi, Murid, Mauripur and several other locations. For the first time in this conflict Hunters went into action in East Pakistan, knocking out an air defence command post and radar station with rocket and cannon fire. In the west, other Hunters were involved in attacks on Pakistani artillery positions in Kashmir. Six Hunters were lost during the day's operations; one of them fell victim to intense ground fire, two to MiG-19s and the other three to Dassault Mirages. One Mirage pilot claimed the destruction of two Hunters with Sidewinder missiles, but one of them was subsequently awarded to his wing man. The same pilot also claimed to have damaged two Hunters with his 30mm cannon. Also on 5 December, Hunters — accompanied by Russian-built Sukhoi Su-7s — made 31 sorties against troops and artillery positions in the Jessore sector, a HQ at Bogra, railway stations near Santahar and the railway bridge over the River Seasta.

The following day, Hunters carried out a major attack on oil refineries at Karachi and Attock, creating — according to IAF post-strike reconnaissance reports — 'the biggest blaze ever seen in southern Asia'. One Hunter was admittedly lost to ground fire in the Chhamb region, although curiously the Pakistanis made no claim for it. On the eastern front, a Hunter shot down one of the few remaining Sabres in that area.

Intensive ground-attack operations continued on 7 and 8 December. Two Hunters were lost on the 8th, both of them brought down by ground fire, and another was brought down by a 40mm anti-aircraft battery on the 9th during an attack on Pakistani positions at Sulemanki. The next day saw the start of a big Pakistani counter-attack in the Chhamb sector, supported by tanks and aircraft; the latter carried out several attacks on IAF airfields, and during one of these a Hunter was destroyed by a strafing Mirage on the ground at Pathankot. No Hunter losses were recorded between 11 and 14 December, during which period the IAF ground-attack squadrons operated at maximum effort in support of the Indian forces fighting hard to contain the Pakistani armoured thrust; on the eastern front, the Hunters of No 14 Squadron were engaged in attacks on enemy troop and vehicle concentrations to the west of Gorashat, and on the 12th this unit commenced operations from the newly-captured airfield of Jessore.

There were several air combats on 15 December, during which IAF Hunters claimed to have shot down a Pakistani MiG-19 and an F-86. On the debit side, one Hunter was shot down by a Sabre over Rajisthan. That evening, Hunters and Canberras carried out a dusk attack on port installations at Karachi, while on the eastern front the Hunters of No 14 Squadron and other ground-attack aircraft carried out some 40 sorties against Pakistani troops entrenched in the grounds of Dacca University.

There were no further recorded Hunter losses before hostilities ended in the afternoon of 17 December. Documented losses involving Hunters in the two-week war of 1971 were as follows:

Hunter losses December 1971

Date	Remarks
4	Shot down into the sea by an F-86 following attack on Masroor.
4	Hunter serial No A-490 shot down over Murid by F-86. Wreckage photographed by PakAF.
4	Unidentified Hunter shot down by F-86 over Peshawar. Confirmed by cine film and visual reports.
4	Hunter serial No A-462 shot down by F-86 over Peshawar. Wreckage photographed by PakAF.
4	Hunter serial No A-479 shot down by MiG-19 (F-6) over Sakesar. Pilot captured; wreckage photographed by PakAF.
5	Unidentified Hunter shot down near Lahore by Mirage. Confirmed by cine film and visual reports.
5	Unidentified Hunter shot down near Lahore by Mirage. Confirmed by cine film and visual reports.

5	Hunter serial No A-1014 shot down by Mirage over Sakesar. Wreckage photographed by PakAF.
5	Hunter serial No A-482 shot down over Sakesar by MiG-19 (F-6). Wreckage photographed by PakAF.
5	Hunter serial No A-488 shot down over Sakesar by MiG-19. Wreckage photographed by PakAF.
5	Unidentified Hunter shot down by ground fire over Chor (Sind). Pilot ejected over Indian territory.
7	Unidentified Hunter shot down by F-86 over Farilka region. Confirmed by cine film and visual reports.
8	Unidentified Hunter shot down by ground fire over Sulemanki. Aircraft crashed in a minefield and could not be photographed.
8	Unidentified Hunter destroyed over Risalawala by ground fire. Loss admitted by Indian AF.
9	Unidentified Hunter shot down by ground fire over Sulemanki. Loss admitted by IAF.
10	Unidentified Hunter destroyed on ground during strafing attack by Mirage on Pathankot. Confirmed by cine film.
15	Unidentified Hunter shot down by F-86 in Rajisthan sector. Confirmed by cine film.

Below: An Indian Mk 56, with a full load of underwing fuel tanks, takes off from Dunsfold on the first stage of the long delivery flight. *BAe-Kingston*

9
RAF Hunters in the Middle East

At the end of 1958, the decision was taken to re-equip No 8 Squadron, Middle East Command's 'resident' strike unit, which was based at Aden, with the Hunter FGA9. At that time, the squadron operated de Havilland Venoms and a flight of Gloster Meteor FR9s and was heavily committed to operations against dissident tribesmen in both the Trucial Oman area and the Western Aden Protectorate.

In mid-1959 a number of pilots were sent to the United Kingdom to convert on to the new type and to bring back to Aden a pair of Hunter T7 trainers, and conversion of the whole squadron got under way in October, being completed without incident by the New Year. Shortly afterwards No 208 Squadron, which had disbanded as a Hunter Mk 6 unit at Nicosia, Cyprus, in March 1959 and subsequently re-formed at Eastleigh, Kenya, with Venoms was warned that it was once again to receive Hunters, and in March 1960 the whole squadron returned to the United Kingdom for conversion to the FGA9 at RAF Stradishall. The Squadron flew out the last of its new aircraft to Nairobi in June and remained there for the time being, although one flight at a time was detached to Khormaksar for armament practice as there was no suitable range in Kenya.

The arrival of the Hunter in Middle East Command raised a number of problems, not all of them of a purely technical nature. Soon after No 8 Squadron re-equipped with the type, the RAF HQ at Khormaksar began to receive complaints from residents of the Aden Colony, who suddenly found themselves subjected to sonic booms at irregular intervals. A 'Boom Flight' system was therefore introduced under which the Hunters were permitted to go supersonic only above 30,000ft while pointing out to sea, after the necessary Air Traffic Control approval had been obtained. The sonic bangs, however, turned out to have an unexpected and beneficial side effect when the Hunters were attacking rebel tribesmen, for they sounded remarkably like a 1,000lb bomb exploding in the distance, which sometimes fostered the impression that an attack was heavier than it actually was. The technique of 'aiming' sonic bangs at rebel positions was used on several occasions to good effect.

Most of the problems encountered by the Hunter units on the Arabian Peninsula were caused by the climate and the primitive servicing conditions. There were very few hangars, which were only just adequate for major servicing, so routine tasks had to be carried out in the open in an atmosphere that was humid and filled with dust and salt. One of the early problems that cropped up involved the Hunter's 30mm Aden gun pack, where the grinding effect of salt and sand produced excessive wear and made necessary the frequent changes of components. Nevertheless, the guns usually worked perfectly well, and instances of stoppages during operational sorties were rare. Inevitably, the nature of the terrain also created problems; airfields which had been suitable for the operation of Vampires and Venoms were only marginally adequate for Hunters, yet the faster jets were often required to operate from them. Inevitably, there were accidents; fortunately, few of them were of a serious nature.

In the summer of 1961, both Middle East Hunter squadrons became involved in a major international crisis when Iraq laid claim to the oil-rich territory of the State of Kuwait and began to move troops and armour in a threatening posture towards the Kuwait border. An agreement already existed under which the British Government was prepared to render military assistance to Kuwait if requested to do so, and a plan — known as 'Vantage' — had been worked out some time earlier for the rapid reinforcement of the area, and in June 1961 another version code-named 'Bellringer' was prepared to encompass the additional forces which had become available in the Middle East since the original scheme was formulated.

Towards the end of June, all forces earmarked for the reinforcement operation were placed on four days' readiness; this was a fairly relaxed state, but Intelligence sources indicated that an Iraqi 'blitzkrieg' on Kuwait was unlikely. However, since the two Hunter fighter/ground-attack squadrons would provide the initial defence of Kuwait against Iraqi tanks and aircraft, it was decided on 30 June to move them both up to Bahrain. For 208 Squadron, in Nairobi, this involved a flight of 2,300 miles; the Hunters set off at first light and covered the 1,000 miles from Embakasi to Khormaksar in two hours, refuelling and setting out for Bahrain after lunch in company with No 8 Squadron. The 1,300-mile flight from Khormaksar was accomplished without incident and by nightfall the Hunter squadrons were dispersed, serviced and fully armed at Bahrain. Although ground support still had to arrive, the Hunters' radius of action was sufficient to take them just beyond the Kuwait-Iraq border, which meant that they were in a position to blunt a sudden Iraqi thrust — albeit in a restricted fashion — even before the Ruler of Kuwait requested full British intervention. Shortly afterwards,

two Canberra B(I)6/8 squadrons (Nos 88 and 213) were ordered from Germany to Sharjah to reinforce the Hunters in the strike role, while two Shackletons of No 37 Squadron arrived at Bahrain and stood ready to carry out flare-dropping operations at night over the potential combat zone.

On the morning of 1 July Royal Marine Commandos were flown by helicopter to Kuwait New

Above: Hunter FGA9s of No 8 Squadron over Salisbury, Rhodesia, during a visit in 1961. *MoD*

Airport, and on that same day the Hunters of No 8 Squadron also flew in from Bahrain and came to immediate readiness. One deficiency in particular caused a great deal of concern at this point; this was

85

the total lack of any kind of warning radar in Kuwait, which would have presented enormous problems for the defending fighters had they been called upon to meet an Iraqi air threat. It was not until 18 July that a portable SC787 radar installation became operational, and even then it was somewhat outdated and left much to be desired. In the meantime, the Hunters relied heavily on the radar of the aircraft carrier HMS *Bulwark*, which was effective up to 80 miles when the vessel stood close inshore. Later, the carrier HMS *Victorious* also provided radar cover.

The lack of suitable radar, however, caused less annoyance and frustration than the operating conditions. Flying conditions were extremely hazardous, with blowing sand cutting down visibility to 400 yards or less, and this led to the death of one 208 Squadron Hunter pilot, Flg Off F. N. Hennessy, who spun into the ground in the forward area. It was believed that he had become disorientated while trying to maintain visual contact with ground positions.

Conditions on the ground, too, were appalling, and both air and ground crews suffered badly from heat exhaustion. It was necessary to maintain one Hunter Flight at 15 minutes' readiness at all times, but the heat made cockpit readiness an impossibility, with cockpit temperatures sometimes exceeding 140°F. A readiness hut was set up close to the flight line in which pilots could wait in their flying clothing, but even after the installation of air conditioning temperatures inside the building often reached 112°F.

By 20 July the Kuwait crisis was considered to have diminished sufficiently to permit the withdrawal of the bulk of the British forces from the area. No 8 Squadron, however, remained at Kuwait New Airport for the time being, while No 208 returned to Bahrain and stood ready to reinforce the other Hunter unit if the need arose. In fact, following the Kuwait crisis a Hunter detachment was always kept at Bahrain (or Muharraq, as the airfield was later renamed) for as long as the British maintained a presence in the area.

One important lesson learned during the crisis was that the two Middle East Hunter squadrons needed to

be brought together to form a single strike wing, and this was created late in 1961 at Khormaksar under Wg Cdr C. R. G. Neville. The two squadrons, which had a combined strength of 32 Hunters and four Meteor FR9s, operated on a rotation basis between Khormaksar and Bahrain, the units spending roughly a month in turn at each location. The primary task of the Bahrain-based squadron was to counter any threat to Kuwait, while that at Khormaksar stood ready to meet any strike commitment in the Aden Protectorates and East Africa.

Soon after the formation of the Khormaksar Strike Wing, at the beginning of 1962, trouble flared up in the Western Aden Protectorate, necessitating further air attacks on dissident villages by Hunters and Shackletons. The air strikes continued at intervals until the end of February, when the dissident tribesmen capitulated. After that, things in the Western Aden Protectorate were fairly quiet until September 1962, when an Egyptian-backed coup overthrew the new Imam of the Yemen and led to the declaration of a republic under General Sallal. A fierce propaganda war, calling for the tribes of South Arabia to rebel against their government, was immediately launched against the South Arabian Federation and Great Britain, and on 22 October several unidentified aircraft crossed into the Western Aden Protectorate from the Yemen and fired rockets at villages in the Naqab area. For some time after that, the Hunters of Nos 8 and 208 Squadrons maintained dawn-to-dusk patrols over the border area, and there were no further incursions by hostile aircraft.

Trouble, however, continued to build up during 1963, particularly in the Radfan, an area some 20 miles long by 15 wide that lies 35 miles north of Aden. Rocky and mountainous, with peaks and plateaus reaching up to 7,000ft, it is split by deep wadis running in all directions and is inhabited by at least 12 tribes, most of whom are fiercely independent and hostile to any outside interference or attempts to administer them. It was these dissident tribesmen who, supported, supplied and encouraged by the Yemen, defied the

Top left: Hunter FGA9 of No 8 Squadron over the Radfan in 1964. *MoD*

Above: Local dignitaries inspecting a Hunter FGA9 of No 8 Squadron, Muharraq, during the Aden crisis of 1967. *MoD*

Right: Ground crew at work on a No 8 Squadron FGA9 at Muharraq. *MoD*

Federal Government in the early 1960s and embarked on a campaign of robbery and murder. Subversion in Aden State itself was also on the increase, and in December 1963 — following an outrage at Khormaksar in which the Assistant to the British High Commissioner was killed and 53 people injured by a grenade — a State of Emergency was declared throughout South Arabia and the frontier with the Yemen closed.

In the New Year, to teach the dissident tribesmen a lesson, it was decided to carry out a demonstration in force — known as Operation 'Nutcracker' — in the Radfan area, operations by security ground forces being backed up by the Khormaksar Strike Wing. The two original Hunter squadrons were now joined by a third, No 43, which had moved to Khormaksar on 1 March 1963 from Cyprus, and there was also a photo-reconnaissance Flight, No 1417, with Hunter FR10s. Because of commitments outside the Radfan

— in other words, the need to maintain a presence at Muharraq — only two of the Hunter FGA9 squadrons would be engaged in 'Nutcracker' at any one time.

Right from the start of the operation, in January 1964, the fighter reconnaissance Hunters of No 1417 Flight played a very important part, producing hundreds of target photographs of the poorly-mapped Radfan area which were then transferred to a large mosaic from which the cartographers were able to work. The Hunter FR10 pilots usually worked under the direction of a Forward Air Controller, as did the ground-attack aircraft.

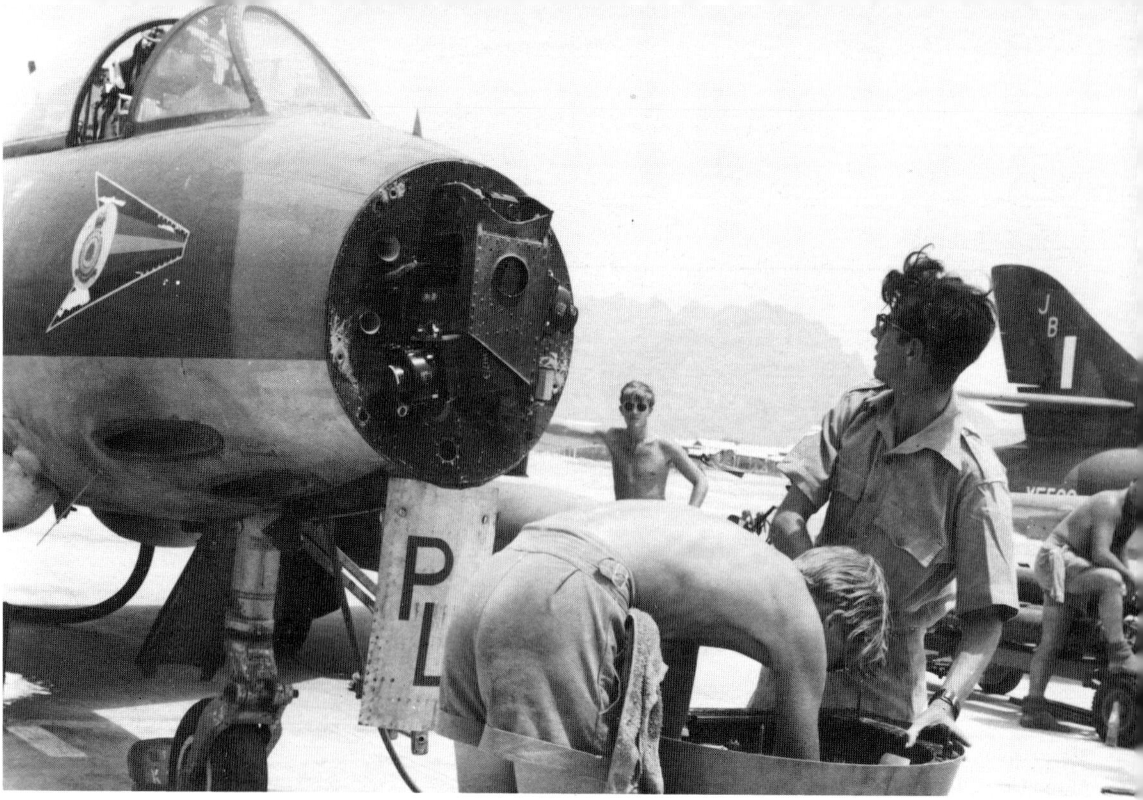
PL
JB

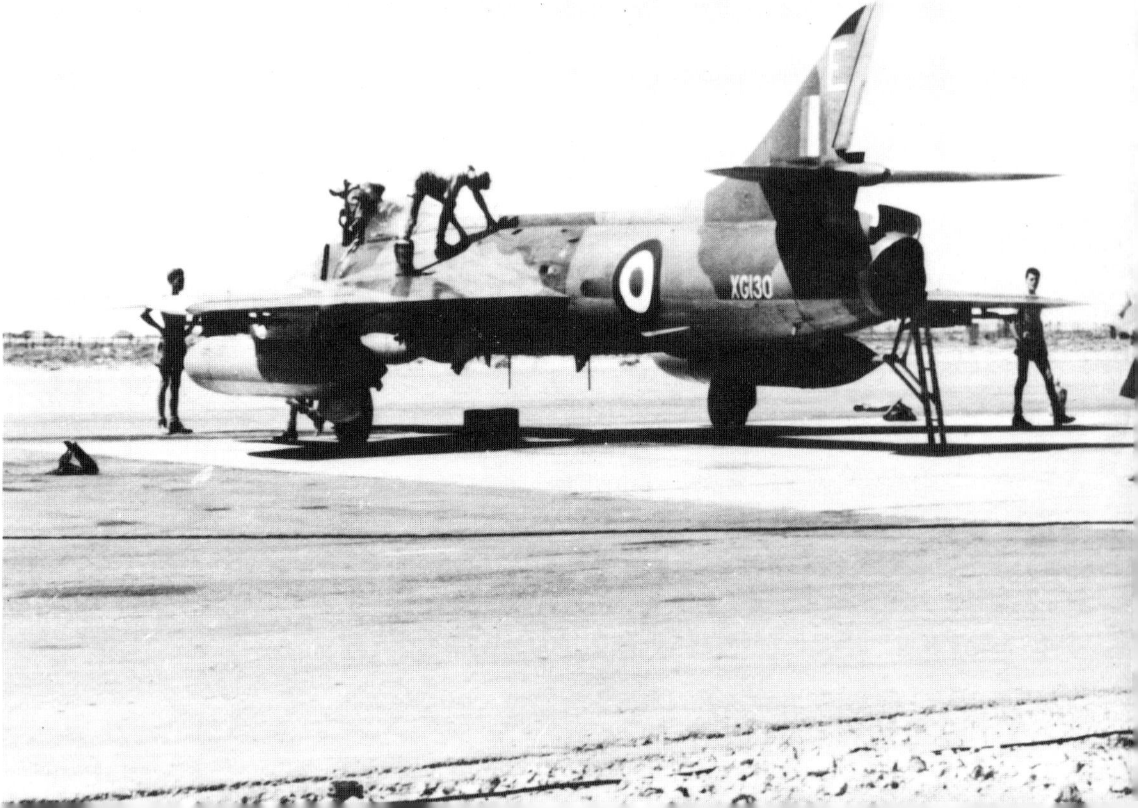
XG130

The Hunter once again showed that it was a strong and reliable ground-attack fighter, but operations in the Radfan tested it to the full, with blown sand infiltrating every crack and blasting windscreens. Flying in a sand haze with a sand-blasted windscreen produced conditions akin to permanent instrument flying, for which the only remedy was frequent windscreen changes.

The Hunters carried out their attacks with 30mm cannon and 3in rockets, the targets being mainly stone fort-type houses and towers, caves and sangars. The pull-out from rocket attacks was often very hazardous in the mountainous terrain and some aircraft inevitably sustained damage from rocket debris, but a very careful check was made on all strikes and cine films showed that in almost every case of damage, the pilot was firing and breaking at the correct range.

The 30mm cannon proved a useful weapon in keeping heads down, and was extremely effective when used for spraying snipers hidden on hillsides. It was also used for target marking under FAC control when

Left: Checking the fire control radar of a Hunter FGA9 of the Khormaksar Wing. *MoD*

Below: Hunter FGA9s of No 1 Squadron on detachment to the Middle East in 1967. *MoD*

the target was difficult to see and smoke was not available from the ground forces. The aircraft fired short bursts in the vicinity of the target and was then directed by the Forward Air Controller; when the target was registered, it could then be attacked by rockets. Usually, such attacks achieved their object fully; a good example was a concentrated rocket and bomb attack on a fort just across the border in Yemen territory on 28 March 1964, when eight Hunters destroyed the building completely as well as wrecking a nearby anti-aircraft gun and several vehicles. Post-strike photography by a Hunter FR10 was so good that warning leaflets dropped before the attack could clearly be seen lying in and around the ruins of the fort when the film was developed.

The Hunters also excelled themselves on 1 May, when a party of 40 soldiers of 22 Special Air Service Regiment were pinned down by heavy sniper fire well inside enemy territory. A radio call for help brought in the Hunters of Nos 43 and 208 Squadrons, which carried out attacks on reported rebel positions throughout the remainder of the day. Eighteen extremely accurate sorties were flown, the Hunters firing 127 rockets and over 7,000 rounds of ammunition before darkness compelled them to break off. The SAS men eventually slipped away during the night for

the loss of two of their number. The following day, the Hunters also provided accurate support for the men of 45 Royal Marine Commando, who had managed to occupy a high and rugged feature known as the 'Cap Badge'; the aircraft strafed rebel positions all day, sometimes to within 150 yards of the Commandos, and it was thanks to this incessant support that units of the 3rd Parachute Regiment succeeded in linking up with the Commandos after a 30-hour action. The Hunters continued to provide effective support during the days that followed, and on occasions they strafed so close to friendly troops that some of the latter were hit by spent cartridges as the strike aircraft flew low overhead.

The stage was now set for the major offensive phase of the whole operation, an assault on the rebel stronghold of Jebel Huriyah. Soon after the advance towards this objective began, on 7 June, ground forces came under heavy fire from across a valley and once again the Hunters were called in. This time, the rebels had made the mistake of fighting a pitched battle from prepared positions, and the casualties inflicted on them by the rocket and cannon attacks were very severe — so severe, in fact, that they were unable to defend the peak of the Jebel, which was occupied at dawn on 11 June.

Although the successful Jebel Hyriyah assault marked the climax of the operations in the Radfan, with the dissident tribes gradually coming in to sue for peace afterwards, a hard core of dissidents still held out in the Wadi Taym area and it was some time before their hideouts could be identified. Once this had been done, Hunters were sent in to destroy them with rocket and cannon fire early in November; the last of the rebels capitulated on the 18th of that month, and that day all offensive action in the Radfan ceased. During the height of the campaign, between 30 April and 30 June 1964, the Hunter FGA9s of the three squadrons involved had flown 527 sorties, launched 2,508 rocket projectiles and fired 176,092 cannon shells, while the Hunter FR10s had flown 115 sorties and fired 7,808 cannon shells.

Top left and centre left: Hunter FGA9 of No 43 Squadron lets fly a rocket salvo during operations in the Radfan, 1964. *MoD*

Left: FGA9 of No 43 Squadron on Middle East detachment, 1964. *MoD*

After their defeat in the Radfan, Yemeni and Egyptian subversive activities switched to the urban areas of Aden State, and terrorism there showed a marked increase after the British Government announced that South Arabia would be granted independence not later than 1968. As far as the RAF was concerned, the main task was to secure Khormaksar against terrorist attack, and an alert system was worked out under which all aircraft except the Hunters would be dispersed in the event of a real emergency. It was necessary for the Hunters to stay at Khormaksar for air defence purposes, for in 1965 Egyptian-flown MiG fighters penetrated the Protectorate on several occasions, attacking villages on the frontier, and air defence patrols by pairs of Hunters from the forward airstrip at Beihan became a regular feature, although no hostile aircraft were intercepted.

The British deadline for withdrawal from Aden, as soon as it became known, also sparked off a resurgence of rebel activity 'up-country' in the Radfan and neighbouring areas, and once again the Khormaksar Strike Wing's Hunters, in addition to maintaining a pair on five-minute readiness at Beihan, were called upon to make frequent air attacks in support of security forces.

By mid-1967, the situation in Aden had deteriorated to an appalling degree, with the Federal Government rapidly losing control to the terrorists, and in August plans were implemented to withdraw the operational RAF presence from Aden to Muharraq. No 208 Squadron's Hunters were already there and they were soon joined by the aircraft of No 8 Squadron. This left only the Hunters of No 43 Squadron at Khormaksar; they were to remain there until completion of the British withdrawal, after which the Squadron was to disband, its aircraft to be distributed between Nos 8 and 208 or returned to the United Kingdom. No 1417 Flight was also to disband, its FR10s being allocated to No 8 Squadron, which was to assume the fighter-reconnaissance task.

In spite of the rapid run-down of squadrons at Khormaksar, intensive flying continued in support of the South Arabian Army, and in September 1967 the Hunters of 43 Squadron flew 142 sorties. The policy now was for a pair of Hunters to remain overhead whenever a RAF or Army Air Corps aircraft was on the ground at one of the up-country airstrips; the fighters would make a low run over the strip to let any nearby terrorists know they were there, then patrol at high altitude to conserve fuel, remaining on call in case the aircraft on the ground was attacked. A further 164 operational sorties were flown in October, after which Sea Vixens and Buccaneers from the aircraft carrier HMS *Eagle* progressively took over the Hunters' air defence tasks.

The last Hunter ground-attack sorties by 43 Squadron were flown on 9 November 1967 against rebels in the Kirch area, bringing to an end the Squadron's four-year service at Khormaksar. The Squadron was then disbanded and its aircraft re-allocated; it eventually re-formed at RAF Leuchars on 1 September 1969 at a Phantom FG1 unit in Strike Command.

The last Hunters to leave Khormaksar were the FR10s which had belonged to No 1417 Flight. Although now on 8 Squadron's inventory, they had been held back at Aden because it had been thought that they might be taken over by a new South Arabian Air Force. This, however, did not happen, so on 28 November they flew to Muharraq to join 8 Squadron. Their departure marked the end of 48 years of RAF presence in the Colony.

Meanwhile, for No 208 Squadron at Muharraq, the mid-1960s had been remarkable only for a routine of constant training, with the odd alert occasioned by the 'accidental' intrusion of Iraqi aircraft into the airspace of Kuwait. In 1966 the Squadron's Hunters received SNEB rocket pods and as a result there was a good deal of live firing practice, although this was restricted to the cooler months because the rocket pods produced problems during periods of high ambient temperature. This was revealed when one of the rockets exploded in its pod, damaging a Hunter, and a subsequent investigation showed that excessive temperature had been the main cause. A restriction of 35°C was therefore placed on the carriage of the SNEB rockets, and a speed of 450kts was not to be exceeded if the temperature was above 30°C.

Other training involved simulated attacks by the Hunters on Royal Navy warships, as well as search and rescue co-operation and anti-smuggling patrols, and in 1967 the Squadron also practised long-range night-flying exercises in case there was a need for the rapid reinforcement of 8 Squadron at Khormaksar. When the latter squadron joined No 208 at Muharraq in the summer of 1967, the two combined to form an Offensive Support Wing, which remained in existence until 1971. Intensive training continued, and although there were no further offensive operations the Hunters carried out a number of goodwill flights, including two by 208 Squadron: one to its old base at Nairobi in December 1968, and the other — early in 1971 — to Peshawar, when four Hunters gave a demonstration of ground-attack procedures to the Pakistan Air Force.

Soon after their return, 208 Squadron, in company with No 8, began to relinquish their Hunters, several aircraft per month being flown back to the United Kingdom as the date approached for the British departure from the Arabian Gulf. No 208 Squadron disbanded at Muharraq (to be reformed on 1 July 1974 as a Buccaneer S2A strike/attack unit at Honington) on 10 September 1971 and its remaining Hunters were handed over to No 8, which progressively returned them to the UK. By the beginning of December only eight aircraft were left, and these flew from Muharraq for the last time on their way home, accompanied by a support Hercules. No 8 Squadron disbanded before Christmas and was reformed on 1 January 1972 at RAF Kinloss as an airborne early warning unit with Shackleton AEW2s.

At 1500hrs on Wednesday, 15 December 1971, the Royal Air Force Ensign was finally lowered at Muharraq. It was the end of an era.

Left and right: FGA9s of No 208 Squadron from Eastleigh, Kenya, practice formation aerobatics with the splendour of Mount Kilimanjaro in the background. *BAe-Kingston*

APPENDIX 1

Hunter Production*

F Mk1 — First production batch of 113 aircraft (Kingston-built)

Serial No	Remarks/Service
WT555	Handling trials; preserved at RAF Cosford (7499M)
WT556	A&AEE Familiarisation
WT557	A&AEE Radio Trials
WT558	Gun firing trials; 54 Sqn
WT559	A&AEE; canopy jettison trials
WT560	Rolls-Royce test bed
WT561	Trial installations
WT562	Trials with one-third span flaps
WT563	Trials with interim flying tail
WT564	A&AEE; interception target aircraft
WT565	Rolls-Royce test bed
WT566	Air brake development aircraft
WT567	A&AEE; gun firing trials; RAF St Athan, serial 7489M
WT568	A&AEE; extended leading edge trials
WT569	Full power aileron trials
WT570	Full power aileron trials
WT571	RAE; area rule trials
WT572	RAE; miscellaneous trials
WT573	Rolls-Royce test bed
WT574	Miscellaneous trials
WT575	229 OCU
WT576	AFDS
WT577	AFDS
WT578	AFDS
WT579	229 OCU; 4 School of Tech Trg, serial 7491M; 2117 Sqn ATC
WT580	43 Sqn
WT581	43 Sqn
WT582	43 Sqn
WT583	43 Sqn
WT584	43 Sqn
WT585	43 Sqn
WT586	229 OCU
WT587	43 Sqn
WT588	229 OCU

*Excluding prototype

Serial No	Remarks/Service
WT589	43 Sqn
WT590	43 Sqn
WT591	43 Sqn; DFLS
WT592	54 Sqn; 233 OCU
WT593	DFLS
WT594	43 Sqn
WT595	43 Sqn
WT611	A&AEE; Avon 115 trials
WT612	A&AEE; Avon 115 trials; RAF Hereford (7496M)
WT613	43 Sqn; DFLS
WT614	Fighter Weapons School
WT615	233 OCU
WT616	A&AEE; engine handling
WT617	DFLS
WT618	43 Sqn
WT619	43 Sqn; 222 Sqn; 233 OCU
WT620	233 OCU
WT621	ETPS
WT622	43 Sqn
WT623	43 Sqn
WT624	229 OCU
WT625	229 OCU; 233 OCU
WT626	229 OCU
WT627	DFLS
WT628	ETPS
WT629	DFLS
WT630	43 Sqn; 222 Sqn; 233 OCU
WT631	229 OCU
WT632	Crashed 8/12/55
WT633	RAE, miscellaneous trials
WT634	222 Sqn; 233 OCU
WT635	233 OCU
WT636	233 OCU
WT637	43 Sqn; 222 Sqn; 229 OCU
WT638	233 OCU
WT639	DFLS
WT640	54 Sqn; 229 OCU
WT641	43 Sqn; DFLS
WT642	43 Sqn; 229 OCU
WT643	43 Sqn; 233 OCU
WT644	43 Sqn
WT645	DFLS
WT646	222 Sqn
WT647	222 Sqn
WT648	222 Sqn
WT649	43 Sqn; 222 Sqn
WT650	222 Sqn
WT651	222 Sqn; RAF Hereford, serial 7532M
WT652	DFLS
WT653	229 OCU
WT654	229 OCU
WT655	233 OCU

Serial No	Remarks/Service
WT656	RAE; trials with blown flaps
WT657	229 OCU; 233 OCU; 54 Sqn
WT658	DFLS
WT659	54 Sqn
WT660	DFLS; 229 OCU; 'Gate guardian' at Carlisle, serial 7421M
WT679	229 OCU
WT680	West Raynham Station Flight; RAE Aberporth (7533M)
WT681	54 Sqn
WT682	54 Sqn; 229 OCU
WT683	DFLS
WT684	DFLS; 229 OCU; 71 MU, serial 7422M; Reading ATC Sqn
WT685	54 Sqn; 229 OCU
WT686	54 Sqn
WT687	54 Sqn
WT688	229 OCU
WT689	229 OCU; crashed 2/9/55
WT690	DFLS
WT691	229 OCU; 233 OCU
WT692	54 Sqn; DFLS
WT693	54 Sqn

Above: Armament trials Hunters in formation including the Fireflash Hunter and XH615, the first prototype T7. Note underwing installation of Firestreak AAMs on XF378 (the P1109B); earlier trials (see bottom photos, pages 18 & 19) involved a fuselage pack. *BAe-Kingston*

Serial No	Remarks/Service
WT694	54 Sqn; DFLS; RAF Debden (7510M)
WT695	229 OCU; 233 OCU
WT696	54 Sqn; 229 OCU
WT697	Demonstration aircraft
WT698	54 Sqn; DFLS
WT699	229 OCU
WT700	229 OCU

F Mk1 — Second production batch of 26 aircraft (Blackpool-built)

WW599	43 Sqn
WW600	43 Sqn; DFLS
WW601	DFLS
WW602	229 OCU
WW603	DFLS
WW604	233 OCU
WW605	233 OCU

Serial No	Remarks/Service	Serial No	Remarks/Service
WW606	222 Sqn; 229 OCU	WN914	257 Sqn
WW607	229 OCU	WN915	257 Sqn; 263 Sqn
WW608	DFLS	WN916	AFDS
WW609	233 OCU	WN917	257 Sqn
WW610	54 Sqn; Fighter Weapons School	WN918	257 Sqn
WW632	229 OCU; RAF St Athan (6516M)	WN919	257 Sqn, 263 Sqn; also used by 1 Sqn for conversion, April 1955
WW633	DFLS	WN920	AFDS
WW634	229 OCU	WN921	263 Sqn
WW635	DFLS; crashed 8/2/55	WN943	257 Sqn
WW636	54 Sqn; 229 OCU	WN944	263 Sqn
WW637	229 OCU; 233 OCU; RAF St Athan (7518M)	WN945	257 Sqn
WW638	247 Sqn, DFLS	WN946	263 Sqn
WW639	DFLS	WN947	257 Sqn; 263 Sqn
WW640	54 Sqn	WN948	257 Sqn; 263 Sqn
WW641	54 Sqn; DFLS	WN949	Damaged beyond repair, 1956
WW642	AFDS	WN950	257 Sqn
WW643	229 OCU	WN951	5 MU; 257 Sqn; 263 Sqn
WW644	229 OCU; RAF St Athan (7521M)	WN952	257 Sqn
WW645	DFLS	WN953	257 Sqn

F Mk2 — One production batch of 45 aircraft (Coventry-built)

WN888	Armstrong Whitworth Aircraft, handling trials
WN889	Armstrong Siddeley Sapphire ASSa12 test bed
WN890	AWA performance trials
WN891	Cold weather trials, CEPE, Canada
WN892	A&AEE
WN893	RAE, miscellaneous trials
WN894	A&AEE
WN895	AFDS; 263 Sqn
WN896	Crashed, 1954
WN897	263 Sqn; 257 Sqn
WN898	257 Sqn; 263 Sqn; 1 Sqn
WN899	263 Sqn; to Henlow as instructional airframe, serial 7542M
WN900	263 Sqn
WN901	257 Sqn
WN902	257 Sqn
WN903	257 Sqn
WN904	257 Sqn; RAF Newton (7544M)
WN905	Crashed, 1955
WN906	AFDS
WN907	257 Sqn; preserved at RAF Colerne (7416M)
WN908	263 Sqn
WN909	257 Sqn
WN910	5 MU, instructional airframe
WN911	AFDS
WN912	263 Sqn
WN913	263 Sqn; 257 Sqn

F Mk4 — First production batch of 85 aircraft (Kingston-built)

WT701	Drop tank trials, Hawker Aircraft Ltd: converted to T8 for Fleet Air Arm, 1964; 764 Sqn; crashed, 23/8/61.
WT702	A&AEE, radio trials; converted to T8 for Fleet Air Arm, 1964
WT703	External stores trials, Hawker Aircraft Ltd; converted to T8 for Fleet Air Arm, 1965
WT704	Hawker Aircraft Ltd, miscellaneous trials
WT705	A&AEE, handling trials
WT706	RAE, handling trials; converted to T62 (serial No 681) for Peruvian Air Force
WT707	AFDS; crashed, 25/1/55
WT708	54 Sqn; FWS
WT709	54 Sqn; crashed, 3/11/55
WT710	54 Sqn; 111 Sqn
WT711	14 Sqn; converted to GA11 for Fleet Air Arm, 1962
WT712	54 Sqn; converted to GA11 for Fleet Air Arm, 1963; crashed 1965
WT713	111 Sqn; converted to GA11 for Fleet Air Arm, 1963
WT714	111 Sqn; 14 Sqn; crashed 18/8/55
WT715	111 Sqn; 229 OCU
WT716	111 Sqn
WT717	North Weald Station Flight; sold to Peru, 1955, serial No 630
WT718	111 Sqn; 245 Sqn; converted to GA11 for Fleet Air Arm, 1962
WT719	43 Sqn; 92 Sqn; 118 Sqn
WT720	74 Sqn; 111 Sqn

Serial No	Remarks/Service
WT721	54 Sqn; converted to PR11 for Fleet Air Arm, 1962
WT722	26 Sqn; converted to T8 for Fleet Air Arm; 764 Sqn
WT723	54 Sqn; 14 Sqn; 229 OCU; converted to GA11 for Fleet Air Arm, 1962
WT734	Sold to Peru, 1955, serial No 638
WT735	Radio trials aircraft
WT736	Engine trials aircraft
WT737	118 Sqn; 4 Sqn; 222 Sqn; 229 OCU
WT738	118 Sqn; crashed, 23/10/55
WT739	111 Sqn; set up Edinburgh/London speed record (717.504mph) on 8/8/55
WT740	54 Sqn; 247 Sqn; 229 OCU
WT741	118 Sqn; converted to GA11 for Fleet Air Arm, 1962; to Singapore as T57A, 1973
WT742	98 Sqn
WT743	118 Sqn
WT744	AFDS; 247 Sqn; converted to GA11 for Fleet Air Arm
WT745	14 Sqn; converted to T8 for Fleet Air Arm; 764 Sqn
WT746	AFDS; RAF St Athan (7770M)
WT747	98 Sqn
WT748	118 Sqn
WT749	247 Sqn; 229 OCU
WT750	247 Sqn
WT751	247 Sqn
WT752	247 Sqn
WT753	118 Sqn
WT754	118 Sqn
WT755	14 Sqn; converted to T8 for Fleet Air Arm
WT756	Sold to Peru, 1955, serial No 639
WT757	118 Sqn; crashed, 20/10/55
WT758	Sold to Peru, 1955, serial No 633
WT759	111 Sqn; sold to Peru, 1955, serial No 642
WT760	118 Sqn
WT761	14 Sqn; 98 Sqn
WT762	247 Sqn; crashed, 7/7/55
WT763	26 Sqn
WT764	54 Sqn; 74 Sqn, 247 Sqn
WT765	Sold to Peru, 1955, serial No 645
WT766	Sold to Peru, 1955, serial No 635
WT767	14 Sqn
WT768	118 Sqn; sold to Peru, 1955, serial No 641
WT769	26 Sqn
WT770	To Sweden for evaluation
WT771	111 Sqn; 222 Sqn
WT772	CA aircraft; converted to T8 for Fleet Air Arm
WT773	Sold to Peru, 1955, serial No 644
WT774	Sold to Peru, 1955, serial No 637
WT775	247 Sqn
WT776	Sold to Peru, 1955, serial No 631
WT777	4 Sqn; 98 Sqn
WT778	26 Sqn
WT779	Sold to Peru, 1955, serial No 643
WT780	TIs and experimental camera installation, Hawker Aircraft Ltd
WT795	247 Sqn; 229 OCU
WT796	Sold to Peru, 1955, serial No 640
WT797	14 Sqn; 111 Sqn; to Switzerland as Mk 58A, 1974
WT798	RAE, performance trials
WT799	4 Sqn; 111 Sqn; converted to T8 for Fleet Air Arm
WT800	Sold to Peru, 1955, serial No 636
WT801	4 Sqn; 229 OCU; to Chile as FGA71, 1973
WT802	98 Sqn
WT803	247 Sqn; sold to Peru, 1955, serial No 634
WT804	247 Sqn; converted to GA11 for Fleet Air Arm, 1963
WT805	130 Sqn; 247 Sqn; converted to GA11 for Fleet Air Arm, crashed 22/3/67
WT806	14 Sqn; converted to GA11 for Fleet Air Arm
WT807	14 Sqn; crashed, 18/8/55
WT808	111 Sqn; converted to GA11 for Fleet Air Arm
WT809	66 Sqn; converted to GA11 for Fleet Air Arm
WT810	54 Sqn; converted to GA11 for Fleet Air Arm; crashed, 1965
WT811	111 Sqn; 222 Sqn

F Mk4 — Second production batch of 100 aircraft (Kingston-built)

Serial No	Remarks/Service
WV253	4 Sqn; converted to T7
WV254	247 Sqn
WV255	26 Sqn
WV256	26 Sqn; converted to GA11 for Fleet Air Arm, 1963
WV257	26 Sqn; converted to GA11 for Fleet Air Arm; to Switzerland as Mk 58A, 1973
WV258	54 Sqn; 111 Sqn; to Singapore as Mk 74B, 1973
WV259	14 Sqn
WV260	Oldenburg Station Flight
WV261	26 Sqn; to Switzerland as Mk 58A, 1974
WV262	247 Sqn
WV263	4 Sqn
WV264	111 Sqn
WV265	26 Sqn; preserved at RAF Newton (7684M)
WV266	4 Sqn; to Switzerland as Mk 58A, 1974

Serial No	Remarks/Service	Serial No	Remarks/Service
WV267	93 Sqn; converted to GA11 for Fleet Air Arm	WV366	43 Sqn; to Singapore as Mk74B, 1973
WV268	93 Sqn; preserved at Manston, serial 7701M	WV367	67 Sqn
		WV368	93 Sqn; 98 Sqn; 118 Sqn
WV269	54 Sqn	WV369	26 Sqn
WV270	54 Sqn	WV370	54 Sqn
WV271	4 Sqn; crashed 23/10/55	WV371	54 Sqn; 74 Sqn
WV272	54 Sqn; to Singapore as TMk 57A, 1973	WV372	222 Sqn; converted to T7; No 4 FTS
WV273	67 Sqn	WV373	98 Sqn; 118 Sqn
WV274	4 Sqn; written off in crash landing, 16/7/57	WV374	RAE; converted to GA11 for Fleet Air Arm
WV275	4 Sqn	WV375	54 Sqn
WV276	A&AEE, engine trials (Avon 121)	WV376	222 Sqn
WV277	14 Sqn; 93 Sqn	WV377	14 Sqn; 26 Sqn; 93 Sqn
WV278	66 Sqn	WV378	222 Sqn
WV279	4 Sqn	WV379	111 Sqn
WV280	RAF College of Air Warfare, Manby	WV380	RAF College of Air Warfare, Manby; converted to GA11 for Fleet Air Arm; to Switzerland as Mk58A, 1972
WV281	54 Sqn; 74 Sqn		
WV314	66 Sqn; 92 Sqn; 222 Sqn		
WV315	66 Sqn	WV381	222 Sqn; converted to GA11 for Fleet Air Arm
WV316	4 Sqn		
WV317	54 Sqn; 247 Sqn	WV382	67 Sqn; converted to GA11 for Fleet Air Arm
WV318	14 Sqn; 26 Sqn; 93 Sqn; converted to T7		
WV319	Damaged, 13/1/56; 5 MU; converted to T8; 764 Sqn; attached to XV Sqn at Laarbruch, 1971, after return to RAF inventory	WV383	Converted to T7, then to FGA9; 28 Sqn
		WV384	71 Sqn; crashed, 5/4/57
		WV385	66 Sqn; Avon 115 trials aircraft
		WV386	222 Sqn; to Singapore as T57A, 1972
WV320	222 Sqn	WV387	43 Sqn
WV321	4 Sqn; 111 Sqn	WV388	222 Sqn; crashed, 25/3/57
WV322	92 Sqn; converted to T8 for Fleet Air Arm; 764 Sqn; 809 Sqn	WV389	66 Sqn; refurbished and resold to Abu Dhabi as FGA76
WV323	43 Sqn; instructional airframe (serial 7686M) with Devizes ATC Sqn	WV390	20 Sqn
		WV391	20 Sqn; crashed, 5/6/58
WV324	43 Sqn	WV392	Linton-on-Ouse Station Flight; crashed 17/7/56
WV325	5 MU, storage, refurbished for resale; to Jordan as FGA73A, 1971	WV393	Linton-on-Ouse Station Flight; to Switzerland as Mk58A, 1975
WV326	54 Sqn; to Chile as FR71A, 1974	WV394	20 Sqn
WV327	111 Sqn; 222 Sqn	WV395	20 Sqn; RAF Cosford, serial No 8001M
WV328	247 Sqn; destroyed by fire on ground, 25/1/56	WV396	20 Sqn; converted to T8C
		WV397	20 Sqn; converted to T8C; crashed 23/11/65
WV329	54 Sqn; 229 OCU; to Switzerland as Mk 58A, 1974	WV398	20 Sqn; to Switzerland as T Mk68, 1975
WV330	54 Sqn; 245 Sqn	WV399	222 Sqn
WV331	5 MU, storage; to Singapore as Mk 74B, 1973	WV400	66 Sqn; refurbished and resold to Abu Dhabi as FGA76
WV332	67 Sqn; 234 Sqn; to Switzerland as TMk 68, 1974	WV401	20 Sqn; refurbished for resale to Jorban as FGA73B, 1971
WV333	43 Sqn	WV402	222 Sqn; refurbished and resold to Abu Dhabi as FGA76
WV334	54 Sqn	WV403	67 Sqn
WV363	234 Sqn; converted to T8 for Fleet Air Arm; 764 Sqn	WV404	54 Sqn; to Switzerland as Mk58A, 1974
WV364	26 Sqn; 93 Sqn; 118 Sqn; to Singapore as Mk 74B, 1973	WV405	222 Sqn; refurbished for resale to Switzerland as Mk58A, 1972
WV365	54 Sqn		

Serial No	Remarks/Service
WV406	222 Sqn
WV407	20 Sqn; refurbished for resale to Jordan as FGA73A, 1971
WV408	20 Sqn; refurbished for resale to Jordan as FGA73A 1971
WV409	66 Sqn; destroyed in ground accident, 14/3/61
WV410	20 Sqn; 229 OCU; destroyed in landing accident, 26/3/59
WV411	20 Sqn; refurbished for resale to Switzerland as Mk58A, 1972
WV412	112 Sqn; crashed, 13/9/56

F Mk4 — Third production batch of three aircraft (Kingston-built)

Serial No	Remarks/Service
WW589	20 Sqn; to Switzerland as Mk58A, 1973
WW590	20 Sqn; to Switzerland as Mk58A, 1974
WW591	To Denmark for evaluation; became E-104 in RDAF service

Remainder of this batch transferred to become: Fourth production batch of 20 aircraft (Blackpool-built)

Serial No	Remarks/Service
WW646	111 Sqn; converted to FGA9; 1 Sqn
WW647	98 Sqn; 247 Sqn
WW648	98 Sqn; 247 Sqn
WW649	98 Sqn
WW650	98 Sqn; 222 Sqn
WW651	98 Sqn; 111 Sqn; 222 Sqn
WW652	98 Sqn; 247 Sqn
WW653	98 Sqn; to Chile as FGA71, 1974
WW654	98 Sqn; converted to GA11 for Fleet Air Arm
WW655	98 Sqn
WW656	98 Sqn
WW657	118 Sqn
WW658	98 Sqn
WW659	247 Sqn; converted to GA11 for Fleet Air Arm; to Switzerland as Mk58A, 1973
WW660	118 Sqn
WW661	Converted to T8; 764 Sqn
WW662	Sold to Peru; serial No 632
WW663	14 Sqn
WW664	26 Sqn; converted in 1957 to prototype T8, and later to T8B; to Singapore as T Mk75, 1969
WW665	247 Sqn

F Mk4 — Fifth production batch of 100 aircraft (Blackpool-built)

Serial No	Remarks/Service
XE657	14 Sqn
XE658	54 Sqn
XE659	54 Sqn; 66 Sqn; 92 Sqn; to Switzerland as Mk58A, 1975
XE660	247 Sqn; crashed 5/12/56
XE661	54 Sqn
XE662	247 Sqn; written off after crash landing, 25/5/57
XE663	4 Sqn; 43 Sqn
XE664	26 Sqn; converted to T8; 764 Sqn; to Singapore as TMk75, 1970
XE665	118 Sqn; converted to T8; 764 Sqn
XE666	4 Sqn
XE667	4 Sqn; 98 Sqn
XE668	4 Sqn; 26 Sqn; converted to GA11, 1964
XE669	98 Sqn; crashed, 4/12/56
XE670	26 Sqn; 93 Sqn
XE671	54 Sqn; crashed 1/5/56
XE672	112 Sqn
XE673	112 Sqn; converted to GA11, 1962
XE674	112 Sqn; converted to GA11; to Switzerland as Mk58A, 1973
XE675	26 Sqn; 93 Sqn
XE676	222 Sqn
XE677	93 Sqn; 229 OCU; preserved at Loughborough College
XE678	222 Sqn; to Switzerland as Mk58A, 1974
XE679	111 Sqn; to Singapore as Mk74B, 1973
XE680	130 Sqn; converted to GA11 for Fleet Air Arm
XE681	66 Sqn
XE682	118 Sqn; converted to GA11 for Fleet Air Arm
XE683	54 Sqn; 74 Sqn
XE684	4 Sqn; 98 Sqn
XE685	93 Sqn; 98 Sqn; converted to GA11 for FAA
XE686	AFDS
XE687	118 Sqn
XE688	222 Sqn
XE689	67 Sqn; converted to GA11 for FAA
XE702	A&AEE; to Switzerland as T Mk68, 1975
XE703	4 Sqn
XE704	112 Sqn; to Chile as T Mk72, 15/2/74
XE705	43 Sqn; 92 Sqn; 111 Sqn; written off in crash landing, 3/1056
XE706	43 Sqn; 92 Sqn
XE707	93 Sqn; converted to GA11 for Fleet Air Arm, 1964
XE708	14 Sqn
XE709	222 Sqn
XE710	14 Sqn
XE711	RAF College of Air Warfare, Manby
XE712	222 Sqn; converted to GA11 for FAA, 1962
XE713	66 Sqn
XE714	Bruggen Station Flight

Serial No	Remarks/Service
XE715	3 Sqn
XE716	67 Sqn; 71 Sqn; converted to GA11 for FAA
XE717	67 Sqn; converted to GA11 for FAA, 1963; to Switzerland as Mk58A, 1972
XE718	93 Sqn
XF289	67 Sqn; converted to T8; 764 Sqn
XF290	67 Sqn; crashed, 14/8/56
XF291	67 Sqn; converted to GA11, for FAA 1963
XF292	130 Sqn
XF293	112 Sqn
XF294	130 Sqn
XF295	130 Sqn
XF296	67 Sqn
XF297	130 Sqn; converted to GA11 for FAA, 1962
XF298	130 Sqn
XF299	43 Sqn
XF300	234 Sqn; converted to GA11 for FAA, 1963
XF301	43 Sqn; converted to GA11 for FAA, 1962
XF302	43 Sqn; to Chile as FGA71, 1974
XF303	66 Sqn; refurbished for resale to Switzerland as Mk58A, 1972
XF304	66 Sqn
XF305	67 Sqn; destroyed on ground by fire, 28/11/56
XF306	112 Sqn; to Switzerland as Mk58A, 1974
XF307	112 Sqn
XF308	130 Sqn; to Switzerland as Mk58A, 1974
XF309	112 Sqn; to Kenya as Mk80, 1974
XF310	Experimental Fireflash AAM installation; converted to T8; 20 Sqn
XF311	130 Sqn
XF312	71 Sqn; to Switzerland as Mk58A, 1975
XF313	71 Sqn
XF314	43 Sqn
XF315	93 Sqn
XF316	HQ Flight, 2nd TAF; to Switzerland as Mk58A, 1974
XF317	67 Sqn; to Chile as FR71A, 1974
XF318	118 Sqn; 130 Sqn; to Switzerland as Mk58A, 1972
XF319	66 Sqn; 112 Sqn
XF320	247 Sqn; 229 OCU
XF321	130 Sqn; converted to T7; 56 Sqn
XF322	112 Sqn; converted to T8
XF323	RAF College of Air Warfare, Manby; to Chile as FGA71, 1973
XF324	92 Sqn, 222 Sqn
XF357	130 Sqn; converted to T8
XF358	112 Sqn; converted to T8
XF359	130 Sqn

Serial No	Remarks/Service
XF360	130 Sqn; to Singapore as FR74B, 1973
XF361	130 Sqn; to Switzerland as Mk58A, 1971
XF362	112 Sqn; refurbished and resold to Abu Dhabi as FGA76
XF363	234 Sqn
XF364	130 Sqn; refurbished for resale to Jordan as FGA73A, 1971
XF365	71 Sqn; refurbished for resale to Switzerland as Mk58A, 1972
XF366	112 Sqn
XF367	71 Sqn; refurbished and sold to Abu Dhabi as FGA76, 1970
XF368	4 Sqn; 118 Sqn
XF369	234 Sqn; to Singapore as FR74B, 1973
XF370	4 Sqn; to Switzerland as Mk58A, 1974

F Mk4 — Sixth production batch of 57 aircraft (Blackpool-built)

Serial No	Remarks/Service
XF932	234 Sqn; crashed, 22/9/56
XF933	71 Sqn; to Switzerland as Mk58A, 1974
XF934	234 Sqn
XF935	234 Sqn; refurbished and resold to Abu Dhabi as FGA76
XF936	234 Sqn; refurbished for resale to Jordan as FGA73A, 1971
XF937	112 Sqn; refurbished for resale to Switzerland as Mk58A, 1972
XF938	71 Sqn; converted to T8C
XF939	71 Sqn; converted to T8C
XF940	71 Sqn; 74 Sqn; crashed, 13/10/61
XF941	71 Sqn; to Switzerland as Mk58A, 1974
XF942	71 Sqn; converted to T8C; crashed 6/11/68
XF943	234 Sqn
XF944	234 Sqn; to Switzerland as Mk58A, 1974
XF945	234 Sqn; crashed 20/11/56
XF946	234 Sqn; 3 Sqn; 71 MU; refurbished for display at RAF Bicester
XF947	3 Sqn; refurbished for resale to Switzerland as Mk58A, 1972
XF948	3 Sqn; crashed, 7/11/57
XF949	3 Sqn; destroyed by fire on ground, 13/1/57
XF950	Geilenkirchen Station Flight; to Singapore as T Mk75A, 1973
XF951	3 Sqn; to Switzerland as T Mk68, 1974
XF952	234 Sqn; refurbished for resale to Jordan as FGA73A, 1971
XF953	RAF College of Air Warfare, Manby
XF967	3 Sqn; converted to T8B
XF968	3 Sqn; refurbished for resale to Jordan as FGA73A, 1971
XF969	3 Sqn; to Singapore as FR74B, 1972

Serial No	Remarks/Service	Serial No	Remarks/Service
XF970	Tropical trials aircraft; to Singapore as T75A, 1972	WN962	1 Sqn; 41 Sqn
XF971	3 Sqn; refurbished and sold to Abu Dhabi as FGA76	WN963	41 Sqn
		WN964	41 Sqn
XF972	3 Sqn; to Kenya as FGA80, 1974	WN965	41 Sqn
XF973	92 Sqn; to Switzerland as Mk58A, 1974	WN966	41 Sqn
XF974	3 Sqn	WN967	41 Sqn
XF975	3 Sqn; to Kenya as FGA80, 1975	WN968	41 Sqn
XF976	3 Sqn; to Switzerland as Mk58A, 1972	WN969	41 Sqn
XF977	118 Sqn; converted to GA11 for FAA	WN970	34 Sqn; 56 Sqn
XF978	20 Sqn; converted to T8B	WN971	56 Sqn
XF979	RAF College of Air Warfare, Manby; refurbished for resale to Jordan as FGA73B, 1971	WN972	41 Sqn
		WN973	1 Sqn
		WN974	1 Sqn
		WN975	1 Sqn
XF980	RAF College of Air Warfare, Manby; crashed, 24/8/56	WN976	Wattisham Station Flight
		WN977	1 Sqn; crashed, 5/5/58
XF981	71 Sqn; refurbished for resale to Switzerland as Mk58A, 1972	WN978	34 Sqn
		WN979	56 Sqn
XF982	43 Sqn; to Chile as FR71A, 1974	WN980	263 Sqn
XF983	Oldenburg Station Flight; converted to T8C; crashed 29/6/66	WN981	263 Sqn
		WN982	1 Sqn
XF984	4 Sqn; to Switzerland as Mk58A, 1972	WN983	41 Sqn
XF985	71 Sqn; converted to T8C	WN984	45 MU
XF986	112 Sqn; 234 Sqn; HQ Flight 2nd TAF; crashed 7/8/59	WN985	263 Sqn; AFDS
		WN986	56 Sqn
		WN987	56 Sqn
XF987	83 Sqn; refurbished for resale to Jordan as FGA73A, 1971	WN988	1 Sqn; 41 Sqn
		WN989	263 Sqn; crashed, 23/3/57
XF988	93 Sqn	WN990	263 Sqn
XF989	26 Sqn	WN991	AFDS
XF990	3 Sqn; to Switzerland as Mk58A, 1974	WN992	56 Sqn
XF991	234 Sqn; converted to T8C	WP101	56 Sqn
XF992	43 Sqn; converted to T8C	WP102	56 Sqn
XF993	43 Sqn	WP103	1 Sqn; 41 Sqn
XF994	66 Sqn; converted to T8C; 759 Sqn	WP104	56 Sqn
XF995	247 Sqn; converted to T8B	WP105	263 Sqn
XF996	247 Sqn; crashed, 6/5/59	WP106	56 Sqn
XF997	43 Sqn; crashed, 28/6/56	WP107	263 Sqn; crashed 25/11/56
XF998	54 Sqn; to Switzerland as Mk58A, 1974	WP108	263 Sqn
XF999	54 Sqn; crashed 24/10/56	WP109	56 Sqn
XG341	43 Sqn; refurbished and resold to Abu Dhabi as FGA76, 1970	WP110	56 Sqn
		WP111	34 Sqn
XG342	66 Sqn	WP112	1 Sqn; 41 Sqn
		WP113	1 Sqn; 34 Sqn
		WP114	Engine test bed, Armstrong Siddeley Motors

F Mk5 — One production batch of 105 aircraft (Coventry-built)

Serial No	Remarks/Service	Serial No	Remarks/Service
WN954	A&AEE, high-speed target towing trials	WP115	41 Sqn
WN955	Test bed for Sapphire ASSa7	WP116	1 Sqn; 56 Sqn
WN956	A&AEE, fuel system trials; 1 Sqn; 41 Sqn	WP117	1 Sqn
WN957	RAE, miscellaneous trials	WP118	1 Sqn; 257 Sqn
WN958	A&AEE, external stores trials	WP119	41 Sqn; 257 Sqn
WN959	1 Sqn	WP120	41 Sqn; 56 Sqn
WN960	Damaged and stored, 1956	WP121	1 Sqn
WN961	RAE, miscellaneous trials		

Above: Pictured here while serving with No 1 TWU, Hunter Mk 6A XK149 saw lengthy previous service with AFDS. *RAF Official*

Below: The Hunter's sting — a Mk 6 poses with the enormous variety of stores which the type has carried, operationally and experimentally, during its long career. *BAe-Kingston*

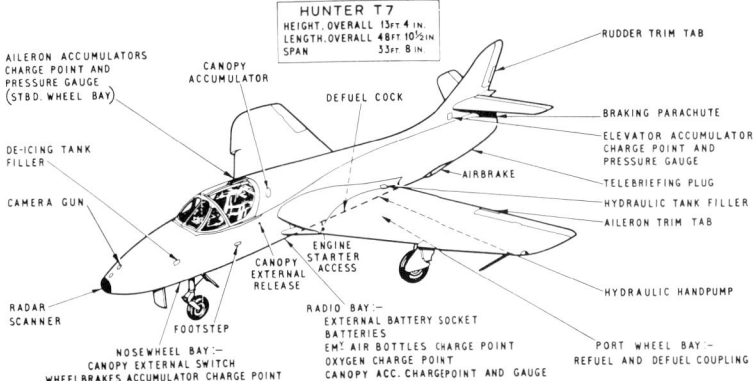

HUNTER T7
HEIGHT. OVERALL 13FT 4 IN.
LENGTH. OVERALL 48FT 10½IN
SPAN   33FT 8 IN

AILERON ACCUMULATORS
CHARGE POINT AND
PRESSURE GAUGE
(STBD. WHEEL BAY)

CANOPY
ACCUMULATOR

RUDDER TRIM TAB

DEFUEL COCK

DE-ICING TANK
FILLER

BRAKING PARACHUTE

ELEVATOR ACCUMULATOR
CHARGE POINT AND
PRESSURE GAUGE

TELEBRIEFING PLUG

AIRBRAKE

HYDRAULIC TANK FILLER

AILERON TRIM TAB

CAMERA GUN

ENGINE
STARTER
ACCESS

CANOPY
EXTERNAL
RELEASE

HYDRAULIC HANDPUMP

RADAR
SCANNER

FOOTSTEP

RADIO BAY:—
EXTERNAL BATTERY SOCKET
BATTERIES
EMᵧ AIR BOTTLES CHARGE POINT
OXYGEN CHARGE POINT
CANOPY ACC. CHARGEPOINT AND GAUGE
ANTI-G SYSTEM CHARGE POINT

PORT WHEEL BAY:—
REFUEL AND DEFUEL COUPLING

NOSEWHEEL BAY:—
CANOPY EXTERNAL SWITCH
WHEELBRAKES ACCUMULATOR CHARGE POINT

Above: XF515, a Mk 6 converted to 6A standard, serving with the TWU, RAF Brawdy; it is seen in this photograph near RAF Cottesmore in 1980. *Brian Lawrence*

Left: Hunter T7 salient features.

Below: GA11s of the Royal Navy's Fleet Requirements Unit on detachment to Gibraltar during NATO exercises. *Peter Gilchrist*

103

Serial No	Remarks/Service
WP122	41 Sqn
WP123	41 Sqn
WP124	34 Sqn
WP125	56 Sqn
WP126	1 Sqn; 34 Sqn; preserved at RAF College, Cranwell, serial No 7569M
WP127	1 Sqn
WP128	Crashed, 1957
WP129	41 Sqn
WP130	34 Sqn; 56 Sqn
WP131	1 Sqn
WP132	34 Sqn
WP133	41 Sqn
WP134	41 Sqn; 263 Sqn
WP135	41 Sqn; crashed, 5/5/56
WP136	34 Sqn
WP137	1 Sqn; crashed, 5/5/58
WP138	1 Sqn; written off 1955
WP139	34 Sqn
WP141	41 Sqn
WP142	34 Sqn
WP143	257 Sqn; crashed, 1956
WP144	1 Sqn; 34 Sqn
WP145	34 Sqn
WP146	1 Sqn
WP147	1 Sqn; 41 Sqn; preserved at RAF Weeton
WP148	41 Sqn
WP149	34 Sqn
WP150	RAE, miscellaneous trials
WP179	263 Sqn
WP180	1 Sqn; 41 Sqn
WP181	263 Sqn
WP182	1 Sqn
WP183	56 Sqn
WP184	34 Sqn
WP185	1 Sqn; RAF Museum, Hendon
WP186	34 Sqn; 56 Sqn
WP187	41 Sqn
WP188	1 Sqn
WP189	263 Sqn
WP190	1 Sqn; 41 Sqn; RAF Upwood, serial No 7582M
WP191	1 Sqn; 34 Sqn
WP192	34 Sqn; crashed, 1957
WP193	34 Sqn
WP194	41 Sqn; 56 Sqn

F Mk6 — One prototype and first production batch of seven aircraft (Kingston-built)

Serial No	Remarks/Service
XF833	Prototype
WW592	A&AEE, handling trials; refurbished and resold to Abu Dhabi as FR76A

Serial No	Remarks/Service
WW593	Hawker Aircraft Ltd, trial installations; converted to FR10
WW594	P1109A; test aircraft for Firestreak AAM; converted to FR10; sold to Lebanon as FGA70
WW595	Trial installations aircraft; converted to FR10; crashed, 24/1/67
WW596	CA aircraft; trial installations; converted to FR10; 2 Sqn
WW597	19 MU, St Athan, 1955; to Jordan as F Mk6, 1958
WW598	CA aircraft; trial installations; to Lebanon as FGA70A, 1975

F Mk6 — Second production batch of 100 aircraft (Kingston-built)

Serial No	Remarks/Service
XE526	Sold to Switzerland, serial No J-4008
XE527	Sold to Switzerland, serial No J-4006
XE528	Sold to Switzerland, serial No J-4009
XE529	Sold to Switzerland, serial No J-4005
XE530	Rolls-Royce test bed; 20 Sqn; refurbished and resold to Kuwait as T67, 1969
XE531	Rolls-Royce test bed; converted to Mk12
XE532	Rolls-Royce test bed; 92 Sqn; converted to FGA9; crashed, 6/5/68
XE533	Sold to Switzerland, serial No J-4002
XE534	RAE, miscellaneous trials; to Lebanon as F Mk6, 1962
XE535	20 Sqn; 26 Sqn; converted to FGA9; 28 Sqn
XE536	Sold to Switzerland, serial No J-4001
XE537	Sold to India, serial No BA233
XE538	Sold to India, serial No BA234
XE539	Sold to India, serial No BA235
XE540	Sold to India, serial No BA236
XE541	Sold to Switzerland, serial No J-4003
XE542	Sold to Switzerland, serial No J-4004
XE543	A&AEE, armament trials; to Jordan, 1958
XE544	66 Sqn; converted to FGA9
XE545	Sold to Switzerland, serial No J-4007
XE546	Converted to FGA9; 43 Sqn
XE547	Sold to India, serial No BA237
XE548	Converted to FGA9; to Rhodesia, 1958
XE549	Sold to India, serial No BA238
XE550	93 Sqn; converted to FGA9; 43 Sqn; to Kuwait, 1967
XE551	A&AEE, miscellaneous trials; to Jordan, 1958
XE552	65 Sqn; 263 Sqn; converted to FR10; converted to FGA9; 54 Sqn
XE553	Sold to Switzerland, serial No J-4012
XE554	Sold to Switzerland, serial No J-4010

Serial No	Remarks/Service	Serial No	Remarks/Service
XE555	Sold to Switzerland, serial No J-4011	XE602	63 Sqn; 92 Sqn; 229 OCU; crashed, 8/3/61
XE556	208 Sqn; converted to FR10; to India as T66E, 1973	XE603	DFLS; AFDS; sold to Jordan as FGA73, 1968
XE557	263 Sqn; to Chile as Mk71, 1971	XE604	263 Sqn; crashed, 2/3/61
XE558	A&AEE, air firing trials; to Jordan, 1958	XE605	A&AEE, trial installations; converted to FR10; to Singapore as FR74B, 1972
XE559	43 Sqn; converted to FGA9 and sold to Rhodesia	XE606	AFDS
XE560	Hawker Aircraft Ltd, trial installations; 43 Sqn; to Rhodesia as FGA9	XE607	263 Sqn; converted to FGA9; crashed, 30/3/62
XE561	19 Sqn; 43 Sqn; 54 Sqn; to Chile as FGA71, 1971	XE608	DFLS; AFDS
XE579	208 Sqn; converted to FR10; crashed, 8/8/61	XE609	54 Sqn; converted to FGA9; 8 Sqn
XE580	208 Sqn; converted to FR10; to Chile as FGA71, 1971	XE610	CA aircraft, Bitteswell; converted to FGA9
XE581	247 Sqn; converted to FGA9; crashed, 22/11/61	XE611	CA aircraft, Bitteswell; converted to FGA9; sold to Switzerland as Mk58A, 1972
XE582	66 Sqn; 247 Sqn; converted to FGA9; 20 Sqn	XE612	74 Sqn; crashed, 17/5/60
XE583	19 Sqn; crashed, 12/9/61	XE613	CA aircraft, Bitteswell; to Rhodesia as FGA9
XE584	1 Sqn; 263 Sqn	XE614	263 Sqn; converted to FR10; to Singapore as FR74B, 1973
XE585	DFLS; converted to FR10; to India as T66E, 1973	XE615	43 Sqn; 263 Sqn; converted to FGA9; refurbished and resold to Singapore as FGA74, 1971
XE586	263 Sqn; crashed, 2/8/57	XE616	263 Sqn
XE587	Demonstration aircraft to Switzerland, 1957; A&AEE; ETPS	XE617	65 Sqn; 92 Sqn; converted to FGA9
XE588	A&AEE, spinning trials; demonstration aircraft to Switzerland, 1957; crashed 9/11/57	XE618	66 Sqn; converted to FGA9; to Kuwait, 1967
		XE619	263 Sqn
XE589	Converted to FR10; to Abu Dhabi as FGA76, 1970	XE620	111 Sqn; 263 Sqn; converted to FGA9; sold to India as Mk56A, serial No A967
XE590	19 Sqn; 263 Sqn; crashed, 10/11/60	XE621	65 Sqn; 92 Sqn; converted to FR10; crashed, 30/1/62
XE591	74 Sqn; refurbished and resold to Saudi Arabia, 1966, serial No 60/602	XE622	263 Sqn; converted to FGA9; 28 Sqn; destroyed by fire on ground, 12/7/66
XE592	43 Sqn; 111 Sqn; converted to FGA9; crashed, 16/10/64	XE623	1 Sqn; 263 Sqn; converted to FGA9; crashed, 11/8/64
XE593	65 Sqn; destroyed by fire on ground, 23/1/61	XE624	263 Sqn; converted to FGA9
XE594	65 Sqn; crashed, 7/3/63	XE625	263 Sqn; converted to FR10; 4 Sqn; to Chile as FGA71, 1971
XE595	65 Sqn; 66 Sqn; crashed, 26/7/57	XE626	263 Sqn; converted to FR10; 4 Sqn; to Kenya as FGA80, 1974
XE596	63 Sqn; 66 Sqn; converted to FR10	
XE597	64 Sqn; converted to FGA9; 208 Sqn; 54 Sqn; 1 Sqn	XE627	65 Sqn; 92 Sqn
XE598	A&AEE, gun blast deflector trials aircraft; to Lebanon, 1958	XE628	111 Sqn; 263 Sqn; converted to FGA9; crashed, 24/4/63
XE599	Hawker Aircraft Ltd, leading edge extensions; 208 Sqn; converted to FR10; to Singapore as FGA74B, 1973	XE643	63 Sqn; 66 Sqn; converted to FGA9
		XE644	65 Sqn; 92 Sqn; to Chile as FGA71, 1971
		XE645	63 Sqn; 66 Sqn; converted to FGA9; 208 Sqn; to Jordan as FGA71, 1967
XE600	Sold to India, serial No BA239; later returned to Hawkers for nosewheel brake trials; crashed, 25/6/62	XE646	1 Sqn; converted to FGA9; crashed, 30/12/66
XE601	Hawker Aircraft Ltd, trial installations; A&AEE, 1971	XE647	63 Sqn; 92 Sqn; crashed, 30/6/64
		XE648	63 Sqn; 66 Sqn

Serial No	Remarks/Service
XE649	65 Sqn; 92 Sqn; 111 Sqn; converted to FGA9
XE650	263 Sqn; converted to FGA9; 1 Sqn
XE651	63 Sqn; 66 Sqn; converted to FGA9
XE652	66 Sqn; DFLS; converted to FGA9; 20 Sqn; to Singapore as FGA76, 1971
XE653	Converted to FGA9
XE654	65 Sqn; 92 Sqn; converted to FGA9; crashed, 20/11/67
XE655	63 Sqn; 92 Sqn; converted to FGA9; to Jordan as FGA73, 1968
XE656	65 Sqn; 92 Sqn; DFLS; 299 OCU

F Mk6 — Third production batch of 110 aircraft (Kingston-built)

Serial No	Remarks/Service
XG217	63 Sqn; 66 Sqn; converted to FR10; to Switzerland as Mk58A, 1971
XG128	20 Sqn; 65 Sqn; DFLS; converted to FGA9
XG129	43 Sqn; 111 Sqn; refurbished for resale to India as Mk56A
XG130	63 Sqn; 66 Sqn; converted to FGA9
XG131	Experimentally fitted with tip tanks by Hawkers; 14 Sqn
XG132	AFDS; to Jordan, 1962
XG133	19 Sqn; 263 Sqn; crashed, 7/9/58
XG134	63 Sqn; converted to FGA9; 208 Sqn; crashed, 16/7/61
XG135	263 Sqn; converted to prototype FGA9
XG136	AFDS; converted to FGA9; crashed, 19/10/64
XG137	92 Sqn; DFLS; to Jordan as FGA73, 1968
XG150	Sold to India, serial No BA247
XG151	54 Sqn; converted to FGA9; 1 Sqn
XG152	DFLS; converted to FGA9; used by No 237 (Buccaneer) OCU, RAF Honington, 1980
XG153	66 Sqn; 92 Sqn; DFLS; converted to FGA9; 20 Sqn
XG154	66 Sqn; converted to FGA9; 8 Sqn; 43 Sqn
XG155	54 Sqn; refurbished for resale
XG156	54 Sqn
XG157	54 Sqn; crashed, 16/6/66
XG158	65 Sqn
XG159	19 Sqn; 263 Sqn; to Jordan as FGA73, 1968
XG160	43 Sqn; 111 Sqn
XG161	AFDS, DFLS
XG162	111 Sqn; DFLS; crashed, 7/11/57
XG163	Sold to India; serial No BA248
XG164	Converted to FGA9
XG165	208 Sqn; crashed, 18/4/58
XG166	14 Sqn; 229 OCU; crashed, 17/2/64

Serial No	Remarks/Service
XG167	19 Sqn; sold to Lebanon, 1958
XG168	Converted to FR10; 79 Sqn
XG169	19 Sqn; converted to FGA9; sold to Singapore as Mk74
XG170	43 Sqn; 111 Sqn; refurbished for resale to India as Mk56A, 1969
XG171	43 Sqn; 111 Sqn; 263 Sqn
XG172	19 Sqn
XG185	19 Sqn; 1 TWU; crashed, 21/4/76
XG186	66 Sqn; 92 Sqn; refurbished for resale to India as Mk56A, 1969
XG187	63 Sqn; 66 Sqn; to Jordan, 1962
XG188	19 Sqn; crashed, 15/5/61
XG189	111 Sqn; refurbished for resale to India as Mk56A, 1969
XG190	43 Sqn; 111 Sqn; refurbished for resale to India as Mk56A, 1969
XG191	19 Sqn; 263 Sqn
XG192	DFLS; FTU RAF Benson
XG193	43 Sqn; 111 Sqn; crashed, 10/6/60
XG194	43 Sqn; 111 Sqn; 1 TWU
XG195	19 Sqn
XG196	19 Sqn; converted to FGA9; 229 OCU, 1975
XG197	DFLS; 1 TWU
XG198	74 Sqn; 111 Sqn; 263 Sqn; 229 OCU; crashed, 4/9/67
XG199	19 Sqn; converted to FGA9; refurbished and resold to Chile as Mk71
XG200	43 Sqn; 111 Sqn; crashed, 1967
XG201	43 Sqn; 111 Sqn; refurbished for resale to India as Mk56A, 1968
XG202	66 Sqn; crashed, 13/2/57
XG203	43 Sqn; 111 Sqn; crashed, 30/4/57
XG204	DFLS; crashed, 15/8/69
XG205	43 Sqn; 263 Sqn; refurbished for resale to Singapore as Mk74A, 1971
XG206	DFLS; crashed, 2/6/65
XG207	1 Sqn
XG208	93 Sqn; crashed, 24/3/59
XG209	111 Sqn; DFLS
XG210	14 Sqn; 66 Sqn
XG211	92 Sqn; refurbished for resale to India as Mk56A, 1969
XG225	20 Sqn; 74 Sqn; 92 Sqn
XG226	66 Sqn; 92 Sqn
XG227	92 Sqn; 111 Sqn
XG228	92 Sqn; converted to FGA9; 229 OCU
XG229	74 Sqn; converted to FGA9; 1 Sqn; crashed, 3/9/71
XG230	92 Sqn; crashed, 15/11/56
XG231	74 Sqn; 111 Sqn; refurbished for resale to Jordan, 1967

Serial No	Remarks/Service
XG232	92 Sqn; refurbished and sold to Chile as Mk71
XG233	66 Sqn; 92 Sqn; crashed, 20/8/58
XG234	74 Sqn; 92 Sqn; refurbished and resold to Jordan as FGA73A
XG235	74 Sqn; 92 Sqn; crashed, 1967
XG236	66 Sqn; crashed, 14/2/58
XG237	66 Sqn; converted to FGA9; refurbished and sold to Jordan as FGA73A
XG238	74 Sqn; 92 Sqn; crashed, 5/5/61
XG239	92 Sqn; crashed, 11/1/58
XG251	66 Sqn; converted to FGA9; refurbished and sold to Singapore as Mk74
XG252	66 Sqn; 92 Sqn; converted to FGA9
XG253	66 Sqn; converted to FGA9
XG254	54 Sqn; converted to FGA9
XG255	66 Sqn; to Jordan as FGA73; 1967
XG256	66 Sqn; converted to FGA9
XG257	66 Sqn
XG258	93 Sqn; crashed, 17/5/57
XG259	54 Sqn
XG260	54 Sqn; converted to FGA9; refurbished and sold to Singapore as Mk74
XG261	54 Sqn; converted to FGA9
XG262	4 Sqn; converted to FGA9; 54 Sqn
XG263	4 Sqn
XG264	54 Sqn; 111 Sqn; converted to FGA9; 54 Sqn
XG265	66 Sqn; converted to FGA9; 20 Sqn; crashed, 1/3/64
XG266	66 Sqn; to Singapore as FR74B, 1972
XG267	4 Sqn
XG268	4 Sqn
XG269	4 Sqn
XG270	4 Sqn; crashed, 28/6/57
XG271	54 Sqn; 63 Sqn; destroyed by fire on ground, 25/7/61
XG272	20 Sqn; 93 Sqn; converted to FGA9 with modified nose to carry F95 camera; refurbished and sold to Singapore as Mk74
XG273	54 Sqn; crashed, 1960
XG274	14 Sqn; 229 OCU
XG289	93 Sqn; crashed, 29/10/57
XG290	A&AEE, miscelleneous trials
XG291	14 Sqn; converted to FGA9
XG292	14 Sqn; 26 Sqn; refurbished for resale to Singapore as FR74A, 1971
XG293	4 Sqn; 20 Sqn; crashed, 21/4/64
XG294	93 Sqn; to Rhodesia as FGA9
XG295	14 Sqn; to Rhodesia as FGA9
XG296	93 Sqn; converted to FGA9; 43 Sqn; refurbished and resold to Singapore as Mk74

Serial No	Remarks/Service
XG297	4 Sqn; converted to FGA19; 20 Sqn; 28 Sqn
XG298	4 Sqn; to Jordan as FGA9; 1967

F Mk6 — Fourth production batch of 45 aircraft (Kingston-built)

Serial No	Remarks/Service
XJ632	93 Sqn; converted to FGA9; 208 Sqn; refurbished and sold to Singapore as Mk74
XJ633	93 Sqn; converted to FR10; 2 Sqn
XJ634	93 Sqn
XJ635	93 Sqn; converted to FGA9; crashed, 4/5/76
XJ636	4 Sqn; 26 Sqn; 1 TWU; crashed, 26/10/76
XJ637	4 Sqn; 229 OCU
XJ638	4 Sqn; to Rhodesia as FGA9
XJ639	4 Sqn; converted to FGA9; 229 OCU
XJ640	4 Sqn; refurbished for resale to Lebanon as FGA70A, 1977
XJ641	93 Sqn; crashed, 11/11/39
XJ642	14 Sqn; converted to FGA9; sold to Singapore as Mk74
XJ643	14 Sqn; converted to FGA9; sold to Singapore as Mk74
XJ644	14 Sqn; to Lebanon as FGA70A, 1977
XJ645	93 Sqn; sold to Jordan as FGA73A, 1969
XJ646	14 Sqn; 66 Sqn; to India as Mk56A, 1969
XJ673	14 Sqn; 66 Sqn; converted to FGA9; 20 Sqn
XJ674	4 Sqn
XJ675	93 Sqn; crashed, 8/1/60
XJ676	93 Sqn; 2 Sqn; 229 OCU
XJ677	Sold to Iraq, serial No 394
XJ678	Sold to Iraq, serial No 395
XJ679	Sold to Iraq, serial No 396
XJ680	20 Sqn; converted to FGA9; sold to Singapore as Mk74, 1971
XJ681	Sold to Iraq, serial No 397
XJ682	Sold to Iraq, serial No 398
XJ683	93 Sqn; converted to FGA9
XJ684	29 Sqn; converted to FGA9; 43 Sqn; sold to Singapore as Mk74, 1970
XJ685	20 Sqn; converted to FGA9; sold to Singapore as Mk74, 1970
XJ686	20 Sqn
XJ687	66 Sqn; converted to FGA9; 208 Sqn; No 1 Tactical Weapons Unit, RAF Brawdy, 1980
XJ688	20 Sqn; converted to FGA9; 208 Sqn
XJ689	14 Sqn; 66 Sqn; refurbished for resale to Singapore as FR74A, 1971
XJ690	14 Sqn; converted to FGA9
XJ691	14 Sqn; 66 Sqn; converted to FGA9; 208 Sqn; crashed, April 1967

Serial No	Remarks/Service
XJ692	20 Sqn; converted to FGA9; sold to India as Mk56A, serial No A969
XJ693	20 Sqn; crashed, 3/10/60
XJ694	CA aircraft, Dunsfold, 1957; converted to FGA9; 208 Sqn; converted to FR10; to India as T66E, 1973
XJ695	20 Sqn; converted to FGA9; No 1 TWU, 1976
XJ712	20 Sqn; refurbished and resold to Saudi Arabia, 1966, serial No 60/601
XJ713	20 Sqn; refurbished and resold to Chile as Mk71, 1970
XJ714	Tropical trials aircraft, Libya, 1957; converted to FR10; sold to Singapore as FR74B, 1973
XJ715	111 Sqn; refurbished and resold to Saudi Arabia, 1966, serial No 60/604
XJ716	20 Sqn; sold to Rhodesia as FGA9
XJ717	20 Sqn; 93 Sqn; sold to Chile as FR71A, 1968
XJ718	93 Sqn; sold to Rhodesia as FGA9

F Mk6 — Fifth production batch of 53 aircraft (Kingston-built)

Serial No	Remarks/Service
XK136	74 Sqn; converted to FGA9; 20 Sqn; crashed, 19/10/64
XK137	20 Sqn; converted to FGA9; 43 Sqn
XK138	14 Sqn; 20 Sqn
XK139	66 Sqn; converted to FGA9; 1 Sqn; 208 Sqn
XK140	74 Sqn; converted to FGA9; 8 Sqn
XK141	74 Sqn; 229 OCU
XK142	74 Sqn; converted to FGA9; 20 Sqn; sold to Singapore as FR74B, 1972
XK143	Sold to Iraq, serial No 400
XK144	Sold to Iraq, serial No 401
XK145	Sold to Iraq, serial No 402
XK146	Sold to Iraq, serial No 403
XK147	Sold to Iraq, serial No 404
XK148	A&AEE trials aircraft; sold to Chile as FR71A, 1968
XK149	AFDS; 1 Sqn; 54 Sqn
XK150	AFDS; converted to FGA9; sold to Jordan, 1968
XK151	AFDS; converted to FGA9; 8 Sqn; 2 Tactical Weapons Unit; crashed, 12/2/80, on Isle of Skye
XK152	Sold to Iraq, serial No 405
XK153	Sold to Iraq, serial No 406
XK154	Sold to Iraq, serial No 407
XK155	Sold to Iraq, serial No 408
XK156	Sold to Iraq, serial No 409

Serial No	Remarks/Service
XK157-XK224:	Sold to India as Mk56s; Indian Air Force serials BA201-BA232

F Mk6 — Production batch of 100 aircraft (Armstrong-Whitworth Aircraft Ltd, Coventry-built)

Serial No	Remarks/Service
XF373	Converted to FGA9; sold to Jordan, 1958
XF374	Converted to FGA9 for Rhodesia
XF375	A&AEE; ETPS
XF376	Converted to FGA9
XF377	Converted to FGA9; sold to Lebanon, 1958
XF378	Firestreak trials aircraft (P1109B)
XF379	Converted to FGA9; sold to Jordan, 1958
XF380	Converted to FGA9; sold to Jordan, 1958
XF381	Converted to FGA9; sold to Jordan, 1958
XF382	65 Sqn; 92 Sqn
XF383	1 Sqn; 65 Sqn
XF384	92 Sqn; 111 Sqn; 299 OCU; crashed, 10/8/72
XF385	65 Sqn; 92 Sqn
XF386	65 Sqn; 92 Sqn
XF387	Converted to FGA9; 229 OCU; crashed, 10/8/72
XF388	65 Sqn; converted to FGA9
XF389	92 Sqn; refurbished and sold to Jordan as FGA73A
XF414	56 Sqn; 63 Sqn; converted to FGA9; crashed, 20/2/67
XF415	Converted to FGA9; sold to Jordan, 1962
XF416	43 Sqn; 111 Sqn
XF417	Converted to FGA9
XF418	229 OCU
XF419	74 Sqn; converted to FGA9
XF420	Converted to FGA9; 54 Sqn
XF421	54 Sqn; converted to FGA9; 208 Sqn
XF422	Converted to FR10
XF423	Converted to FGA9
XF424	43 Sqn; 111 Sqn; converted to FGA9
XF425	74 Sqn; crashed, 26/8/59
XF426	Converted to FR10; sold to Oman, 1976
XF427	54 Sqn; crashed, 13/3/57
XF428	208 Sqn; converted to FR10; sold to Singapore as FR74B, 1972
XF429	Prototype FR10; sold to Switzerland as Mk58A, 1974
XF430	43 Sqn; 111 Sqn; refurbished for resale to Lebanon as FGA70A
XF431	54 Sqn; converted to FGA9
XF432	Converted to FR10; sold to Singapore as FR74B, 1972
XF433	65 Sqn; 263 Sqn; crashed, 7/3/63
XF434	43 Sqn; 247 Sqn; crashed, 11/4/60

Serial No	Remarks/Service	Serial No	Remarks/Service
XF435	43 Sqn; 247 Sqn; converted to FGA9; 8 Sqn	XF507	65 Sqn
		XF508	54 Sqn; 111 Sqn
XF436	Converted to FR10; sold to Switzerland as Mk58A, 1972	XF509	54 Sqn; to RAE for use as chase aircraft in hypersonic flight programme
XF437	43 Sqn; 247 Sqn; sold to Singapore as FR74A, 1971	XF510	Crashed, 30/7/57
		XF511	74 Sqn; converted to FGA9
XF438	Converted to FR10; 4 Sqn; sold to Switzerland as Mk58A, 1971	XF512	Refurbished and sold to Chile as Mk71
		XF513	54 Sqn; crashed, 1/9/58
XF439	247 Sqn; 229 OCU	XF514	247 Sqn; sold to Jordan, 1968
XF440	247 Sqn; converted to FGA9	XF515	43 Sqn; 247 Sqn; converted to F6A; Tactical Weapons Unit, Brawdy, 1978
XF441	208 Sqn; converted to FR10; sold to Singapore as FR74B, 1973	XF516	56 Sqn; 92 Sqn; 229 OCU
XF442	247 Sqn; converted to FGA9; used for SNEB rocket trials	XF517	92 Sqn; 111 Sqn; converted to FGA9; 54 Sqn
XF443	65 Sqn; 92 Sqn; 229 OCU; crashed, 3/8/67	XF518	66 Sqn; 92 Sqn; sold to Jordan, 1962
		XF519	66 Sqn; converted to FGA9
XF444	Sold to Jordan, 1958	XF520	92 Sqn; refurbished and sold to Jordan as FGA73, 1968
XF445	Converted to FGA9; 43 Sqn		
XF446	111 Sqn; converted to FGA9; sold to India as Mk56A, Serial No A1010	XF521	66 Sqn; 92 Sqn; refurbished for resale to India as Mk56A, 1969
XF447	65 Sqn; 92 Sqn; refurbished and sold to Chile as Mk71	XF522	92 Sqn; crashed, 11/1/58
		XF523	54 Sqn; converted to FGA9; crashed, 24/6/63
XF448	74 Sqn; crashed, 21/8/58	XF524	111 Sqn; 54 Sqn; crashed, 5/11/57
XF449	263 Sqn; 19 Sqn	XF525	19 Sqn; 111 Sqn; 263 Sqn; crashed, 7/6/57
XF450	Refurbished and sold to Saudi Arabia, 1966, serial No 60/603	XF526	63 Sqn
		XF527	19 Sqn; 66 Sqn; 111 Sqn
XF451	247 Sqn; 229 OCU; crashed, 20/7/62		
XF452	Trials; sold to Jordan, 1958	**T Mk7** *	
XF453	54 Sqn; 247 Sqn; refurbished and sold to Chile as FR71A	XJ615	First prototype; ETPS; written off 26/6/64
XF454	43 Sqn; 247 Sqn; converted to FGA9; sold to Jordan, 1968	XJ627	Second prototype; to Martin Baker Ltd; refurbished and sold to Chile
XF455	43 Sqn; 247 Sqn; converted to FGA9; crashed, 19/9/64	XL563	Trials aircraft; first production T7
XF456	43 Sqn; 247 Sqn; converted to FGA9; sold to Singapore as Mk74	XL564	Trials aircraft; 19 Sqn; A&AEE
		XL565	208 Sqn; 1417 Flight
XF457	Refurbished and sold to Lebanon as FGA70	XL566	Trials aircraft; 43 Sqn
		XL567	229 OCU
XF458	Converted to FR10; 2 Sqn; sold to Singapore as FR74B, 1972	XL568	74 Sqn; converted to T7A
		XL569	229 OCU
XF459	Converted to FR10; sold to India as T66E, 1973	XL570	229 OCU; crashed 29/8/58
		XL571	229 OCU, 92 Sqn
XF460	Converted to FR10; 1417 Flight, Khormaksar; sold to Singapore as FR74B, 1973	XL572	229 OCU
		XL573	AFDS
XF461	Supplied to Lebanon, 1958	XL574	Used for de-icing trials; fatigue tested to destruction
XF462	66 Sqn; converted to FGA9; refurbished for resale to Switzerland as Mk58A	XL575	229 OCU
		XL576	229 OCU
XF463	Converted to Mk56 for India, 1958	XL577	229 OCU
XF495	Supplied to Lebanon, 1958	XL578	229 OCU
XF496-	Sold to Rhodesia after conversion to	XL579	229 OCU
XF505	FGA9, 1963-64	XL583	229 OCU
XF506	111 Sqn; 263 Sqn	XL586	229 OCU
		XL587	229 OCU

Serial No	Remarks/Service	Serial No	Remarks/Service
XL591	AFDS	XL618	Gutersloh Station Flight
XL592	229 OCU	XL619	20 Sqn
XL593	AFDS	XL620	66 Sqn; 74 Sqn
XL594	19 Sqn	XL621	229 OCU
XL595	AFDS	XL622	Jever Station Flight
XL596	54 Sqn; crashed, 7/11/73	XL623	5 MU, storage; then to various units as 'hack' aircraft
XL597	66 Sqn; 208 Sqn		
XL600	65 Sqn		
XL601	1 Sqn		
XL605	92 Sqn; 66 Sqn; converted to Saudi Arabian Mk7; sold to Jordan as T66B; returned to UK; re-serialled XX467; TWU	**T Mk8** *	
		WW664	T8 prototype
		XL580	764 Sqn
XL609	56 Sqn	XL581	Crashed at Lossiemouth, 6/8/58
XL610	111 Sqn; crashed, 7/6/62	XL582	RNAS Lossiemouth/RNAS Yeovilton Station Flights; crashed, 26/1/68
XL611	43 Sqn; converted to T7A; crashed, 14/5/68		
		XL584	764 Sqn
XL612	402 WTU; 43 Sqn	XL585	RNAS Lossiemouth Station Flight
XL613	43 Sqn	XL598	764 Sqn
XL614	402 WTU; converted to T7A; 237 (Buccaneer) OCU, 1973	XL599	764 Sqn; crashed, 23/8/61
		XL602	764 Sqn; converted to T8M for Blue Fox radar trials in connection with Sea Harrier programme
XL615	Khormaksar Station Flight; crashed, 1/6/60		
		XL603	RNAS Lossiemouth/RNAS Yeovilton station flights; converted to T8M
XL616	402 WTU; converted to T7A		
XL617	Jever Station Flight; converted to T7A; A&AEE	XL604	764 Sqn; 759 Sqn; sold to Kenya as T81, 1974

*T7/8 new build — for conversions see Appendix 1.

1 Radar Ranging radome
2 Radar Ranging scanner dish
3 Nosewheel front door
4 Nosewheel retraction bay
5 Windscreen de-icing tank (removed on some aircraft)
6 Pressurised bulkhead (Frame 6)
7 Forward-retracting (castoring and self-centring) nosewheel unit
8 Nosewheel rear door
9 Adjustable rudder bar functioning in conjunction with differential brakes
10 Instrument panel mounted on Frame 8
11 Detachable armament pack containing four 30 mm. Aden gun bodies and magazine in underside of fuselage
12 Throttle lever with Radar Ranging twist-grip control
13 Low pressure fuel cock control
14 Port instrument/control console
15 Ammunition link collector bay
16 Pressurised cabin floor
17 Anti-G air bottles (two)
18 Magazine (ammunition tank containing up to 150 rounds per gun)
19 Cartridge case ejector chute
20 Front transport joint (Frames 18A and B)

21 Radio bay
22 Boundary layer splitter plate
23 Engine air intake integral with stub wing
24 Boundary layer ducts and louvres
25 Air intake pressure relief door
26 Air intake trunking
27 Wing fuel tanks fabricated in flexible rubber reinforced with vulcanised net
28 Outboard drop tank pressurising pipe
29 Fabricated main wing spar
30 Mainwheel retraction bay
31 Mainwheel retraction jack
32 Fabricated rear wing spar
33 100-gallon (454-litre) Bristol phenolic-asbestos drop tank shown at inboard wing station
34 Inward-retracting mainwheel unit incorporating hydraulic wheelbrakes with Maxaret anti-skid system
35 Inboard store pylon
36 Wing leading edge extension
37 Outboard drop tank fuel transfer pipe
38 Aileron control tube
39 Electrically-heated pitot head
40 Port navigation light

41 Detachable wing tip
42 Port aileron
43 Aileron hydraulic booster jack
44 Aileron trim tab (port only)
45 Port split flap
46 Flap operating jack
47 Engine rear mounting trunnion
48 Hydraulically-operated airbrake
49 Removable engine jetpipe
50 Telebrief socket (under fuselage)
51 Electrically-actuated variable incidence tailplane
52 Hydraulically-boosted tailplane
53 Anti-buffet fairing
54 Rudder trim tab
55 Manually-operated rudder
56 Dielectric fin tip and aerial
57 Front (main) fin spar
58 Rudder control tube
59 Engine bay ventilation duct exit
60 Dorsal spine fairing
61 10,000 lb.s.l.s.t. Rolls-Royce Avon Mk. 203 or 209 (R.A.28 rating) axial-flow turbojet
62 Wing root/wheelbay bottom drag member
63 Rear spar frame 32
64 Cabin conditioning hot air exit duct
65 Tail control operating tubes
66 DME azimuth aerials
67 Main spar frame 25

68 VHF radio aerial (both wing tips)
69 Hood fairing with casing for flying controls led up from under cabin floor behind ejector seat
70 Sliding canopy rail
71 Martin-Baker Mk.3H pilot ejector seat
72 Single-piece plastic sliding canopy
73 Double-thickness optically-flat bullet-proof windscreen
74 Gyro-gunsight Mk.8 combining "fixed" and "gyro" sighting system in conjunction with Radar Ranging Mk.1
75 Radar Ranging Mk.1 unit
76 Cooling air pipe for Radar Ranging
77 Cine camera (G.90) and magazine
78 Camera aperture slot and ram air duct entry for cabin and equipment bay conditioning system

Cutaway of the Hunter F6.
Flight

Note: The aircraft shown above is representative of the Hunter F. Mk. 6 in service with the R.A.F. The Mk. 6/Interim Mk. 9 is similar but features provision to carry 230-gall. (1 044 litre) drop tanks on the inboard wing pylons and includes increased oxygen capacity for the pilot. Some aircraft have been fitted with braking parachutes—as incorporated in full-standard Hunter F.G.A. Mk. 9s.

Left: Two F6s (XF389 and XE618), a T7 (XL564) and a T8 (WW664) in formation. The leading Mk 6 was later refurbished and sold to Jordan. *BAe-Kingston*

Below: F51s of the RDAF delivered in the summer of 1956. Both aircraft, serials E410 and E423, were withdrawn from service in March 1974. *RDAF*

HAWKER HUNTER F. MARK 6 SPECIFICATION
Dimensions.—Wing span, 33 ft. 8 in. (10.25 m); length, 45 ft. 10½ in. (13.98 m); height, 13 ft. 2 in. (4.0 m); wing area, 349 sq. ft. (32.42 m²); wing thickness/chord ratio, 0.085 constant; quarter-chord sweepback, 40°.
Weights.—Empty, 14,400 lb. (6 540 kg); A.U.W. (clean), 17,750 lb. (8 060 kg); A.U.W. (with two 100-gall./454-litre drop tanks, 19,700 lb. (8 940 kg); Max. A.U.W. (with two 230-gall./1 044-litre and two 100-gall./454-litre drop tanks), 24,600 lb. (11 170 kg).
Performance.—Max. speed at 36,000 ft. (11 000 m), 630 m.p.h. (547 kts./1 015 km/h=0.95 Mach); Max. speed at sea level, 716 m.p.h. (620 kts./1 150 km/h=0.93 Mach); initial rate of climb at sea level, 17,200 ft./min. (87.3 m/sec); absolute ceiling, 54,000 ft. (16 460 m); time to 50,000 ft. (15 240 m) from wheels rolling, 10.3 min.; take-off ground run in still air (at sea level), 600 yds. (550 m); landing ground run in still air, typical case), 700 yds. (640 m); maximum ferry range in still air, 1,900 st. miles/1,650 n.m./3 060 km.

APPENDIX 2
Basic Data

F Mk1

Span: 33ft 8in
Length: 45ft 10.5in
Height: 13ft 2in
Wing area: 340sq ft
Powerplant: One Rolls-Royce Avon Mk113 turbojet rated at 7,500lb st
Weight: 12,128lb (empty), 16,200lb (loaded)
Max speed: 610kts at sea level, 0.93M at 36,000ft
Service ceiling: 48,500ft
Fuel capacity: 334gal
Armament: Four 30mm Aden cannon in detachable pack under nose

F Mk2

Dimensions: as for F Mk1
Powerplant: One Armstrong-Siddeley Sapphire Mk101 turbojet rated at 8,000lb st
Weight: as for F Mk1
Max speed: 612kts at sea level, 0.94M at 36,000ft
Service ceiling: 50,000ft
Fuel capacity: 314gal
Armament: as for F Mk1

F Mk4

Dimensions: as for F Mk1
Powerplant: One Rolls-Royce Avon Mk113, 115, 119, 120, 121 or 122 turbojet rated at 7,500-8,000lb st
Weight: 12,543lb (empty), 17,100lb (loaded)
Max speed: 610kts at sea level, 0.94M at 36,000ft
Service ceiling: 50,000ft
Fuel capacity: 414 gal (plus additional 400 gal in underwing tanks)
Armament: Four 30mm Aden cannon; variety of underwing stores including 2in rockets, 500lb or 1,000lb bombs, 3in RPs, 100gal napalm tanks

F Mk5

Dimensions: as for F Mk1
Powerplant: as for F Mk2
Weight: as for F Mk4

Max speed: as for F Mk2
Service ceiling: as for F Mk2
Fuel capacity: 388gal (plus additional 400gal in underwing tanks)
Armament: as for F Mk4

F Mk6

Dimensions: as for F Mk1 except for wing area, increased to 349sq ft with leading edge extensions
Powerplant: One Rolls-Royce Avon Mk203/207 turbojet rated at 10,000lb st
Weight: 12,760lb (empty), 17,750lb (loaded)
Max speed: 620kts at sea level, 0.95M at 36,000ft
Service ceiling: 48,900ft
Fuel capacity: 390gal (plus additional 600gal in underwing tanks)
Armament: as for F Mk4

T Mk7 and variants

Dimensions: as for F Mk1 except for length (48ft 10.5in)
Powerplant: as for F Mk4 except for Mk66 (as for Mk6)
Weight: 13,360lb (13,580lb Mk66) empty, 17,200lb (17,420lb Mk66) loaded
Max speed: 603kts at sea level, 0.92M at 36,000ft (608kts and 0.93M Mk66)
Service ceiling: 47,000ft (48,900ft Mk66)
Fuel capacity: 414gal plus 400 gal in underwing tanks (390 plus 660 Mk66)
Armament: One Aden gun under starboard side of nose (two Aden guns under nose Mk66) Underwing stores as for Mk4/6

F GA6

Dimensions: as for F Mk6
Powerplant: as for F Mk6
Weight: 13,010lb (empty), 18,000lb (loaded)
Performance: as for F Mk6
Fuel capacity: as for F Mk6
Armament: as for F Mk6

FR10

Dimensions: as for F Mk1 except for length (46ft 1in)
Powerplant: as for F Mk6
Weight: 13,100lb (empty),18,090lb (loaded)
Performance: as for F Mk6
Fuel capacity: as for F Mk6
Armament: as for FGA9; three nose-mounted cameras

GA11

All data as for F Mk4 except for gun armament, which was deleted. Provision for rocket batteries on underwing pylons; naval radio equipment installed.